TOTALLY CHOCOLATE

60 DELICIOUSLY SEDUCTIVE RECIPES

ERIC LANLARD

PHOTOGRAPHY BY KATE WHITAKER

MITCHELL BEAZLEY

To Paul and Bobby, for
their continuous support.

An Hachette UK Company
www.hachette.co.uk

First published as *Chocolat* in Great Britain in 2013
by Mitchell Beazley, an imprint of
Octopus Publishing Group Ltd,
Endeavour House, 189 Shaftesbury Avenue,
London WC2H 8JY
www.octopusbooks.co.uk

This abridged edition published in 2014

Publisher Alison Starling
Senior Editor Sybella Stephens
Senior Art Editor Juliette Norsworthy
Designer Jaz Bahra
Photography Kate Whitaker
Home Economy Eric Lanlard, Rachel Wood
Recipe Tester Wendy Lee
Prop Stylist Liz Belton
Production Controller Allison Gonsalves

ISBN: 978 1 84533 935 7
Printed and bound in China
10 9 8 7 6 5 4 3 2 1

All recipes have been tested in metric.
Medium eggs and full fat milk should be used,
unless otherwise stated.

CONTENTS

INTRODUCTION

At the age of ten, my attraction to chocolate – the 'food of the gods' – had already started. In fact, my memories go much further back to my family's daily visits to the local boulangerie, where we would buy a brioche and a single bar of dark 'Chocolat Poulain' – the trick was to push the bar up without breaking it and enjoy it on the way to school. The reason that, years later, I chose Le Grand Pâtisserie in Quimper for my apprenticeship is because it was the only local boutique that made its own chocolate!

My fascination with this precious ingredient is still with me and over the years I have made it my mission to discover the history and origins of chocolate, and the techniques of its production. To understand the whole process, from cocoa bean to an indulgent, finished product, I have been lucky enough to walk through a fertile hacienda in South America and a plantation in Trinidad, to touch, taste and smell the raw ingredient and then witness the long process of the cocoa beans being roasted, conched, blended and moulded into delicious chocolate bars, eggs or other fabulous shapes.

But as much as I adore eating chocolate, it's as a baking ingredient that I love it the most and with this book I want to share my passion for chocolate with you. From indulgent chocolate drinks, tarts, muffins and mousses to gâteaux, petits fours and elaborate creations for special occasions, join me in the madness of baking with chocolate!

Eric x

KNOW YOUR CHOCOLATE

HOW TO CHOOSE A GOOD CHOCOLATE

Choosing a good chocolate is first a question of taste. In its raw state, cacao is bitter, so the taste and quality of chocolate depends on the percentage of cocoa solids it contains, the provenance of the cocoa beans and the production process. A good-quality chocolate has a shiny finish and is brittle, with a strong characteristic taste and smoothness, and it should not stick to the palate. A premium chocolate will also have mostly cocoa butter as its main fat content. For baking or making desserts, I personally like to use chocolate with a maximum of 70% cocoa solids, as chocolate with a higher percentage of cocoa solids can be too bitter.

STORING CHOCOLATE

Avoid storing chocolate in the refrigerator – keep it in a cool (15–20°C/59–68°F), dry and dark place away from strong odours like spices, strong foods or other cooking smells.

If your chocolate has a white discoloration on its surface (chocolate bloom), it is best to discard it, as that means it is old or has been stored in extreme temperatures.

WORKING WITH CHOCOLATE

MELTING CHOCOLATE

In a bain-marie
The classic way to melt chocolate is in a heatproof bowl set over a saucepan of barely simmering water. For a great result, the secret is to melt the chocolate gently over a very low heat, making sure the surface of the water does not touch the bowl.

In a microwave
Alternatively, you can put chocolate into a microwavable bowl and zap it in the microwave on high power for few seconds at a time, stirring gently in between bursts, until melted. Every microwave is different, so it is worth testing a small amount of chocolate in your microwave first, to see how long it takes to melt. Remember, milk and white chocolate burn more easily than dark chocolate, so be very cautious and gentle when melting them, whichever process you use.

TEMPERING CHOCOLATE

WHAT IS TEMPERING?

Tempering is a technique that pastry chefs and chocolatiers use to stabilize chocolate and achieve a glossy, hard, brittle finish, making tempered chocolate perfect for dipping individual chocolates and truffles or coating biscuits and cakes. It involves melting and cooling chocolate, then bringing it to the correct temperature for coating.

THE TECHNIQUE

For best results, use a chocolate or sugar thermometer to check that the correct temperature for each stage has been reached.

First, if using a bar of chocolate, chop your chocolate as finely as possible. Melt two-thirds of it in a heatproof bowl set over a saucepan of barely simmering water (see Melting chocolate on page 11). Remove the bowl from the pan when the chocolate is just melted and has reached the required temperature (see chart opposite).

Add the remaining chocolate a little at the time, stirring gently between additions. Continue to stir gently until all the chocolate is melted and the mixture has cooled to 26–27°C (79–81°F) (see chart opposite).

Return the bowl of melted chocolate to the pan and reheat to 28–30°C (82–86°F) (see chart).

To test, drizzle a few drops of the chocolate on to a piece of baking paper – the chocolate should set in a few minutes and be ready for use. If it sets too fast, return the bowl to the pan and heat for a few seconds to make it more fluid. Use for dipping and coating.

Chocolate Tempering Temperatures

Chocolate	Melted Temperature	Cooled Temperature	Reheated Temperature
Dark	50°C (122°F)	27°C (81°F)	30°C (86°F)
Milk	45°C (113°F)	27°C (81°F)	29°C (84°F)
White	40°C (104°F)	26°C (79°F)	28°C (82°F)

FROM THE
BAKERY

CHOCOLATE AND VANILLA MARBLE CAKE

This recipe is one of my earliest baking recipes. I used to make it every Wednesday when I was off school – it's fun and easy to make, and a great teatime treat.

SERVES 8

Preparation time: 15 minutes, plus cooling
Cooking time: 50 minutes

125g (4oz) unsalted butter, melted and cooled, plus extra for greasing
125g (4oz) dark chocolate, roughly chopped
5 eggs, separated
125g (4oz) golden caster sugar
125g (4oz) plain flour
2 tsp baking powder
2 tsp vanilla extract or paste

Preheat the oven to 180°C (fan 160°C)/350°F/gas mark 4. Grease a 900g (2lb) loaf tin and line with baking paper.

Melt the chocolate in a heatproof bowl set over a saucepan of barely simmering water, making sure the surface of the water does not touch the bowl.

In a large bowl, whisk the egg yolks and sugar together using an electric hand whisk until pale. Beat in the cooled, melted butter, then sift in the flour and baking powder and fold in.

Separate the mixture into 2 large bowls. Fold the vanilla into one of the mixtures and the melted chocolate into the other. In a large, clean, dry bowl, whisk the egg whites to stiff peaks, then gently fold half of the egg whites into each cake mixture.

Spoon layers of the mixtures alternately into the prepared tin, then run through a skewer 2–3 times to create a marbled effect. Bake in the oven for 45 minutes, or until a skewer inserted into the centre comes out clean. Leave to cool in the tin for 10 minutes, then turn out on to a cooling rack to cool completely.

TIP

To make the cake even more luxurious, coat it with melted dark chocolate.

CHOCOLATE AND CINNAMON BUNS

When I travel to the USA I always make a point of going to the local bakery or food hall to get some freshly baked cinnamon buns. The aroma is so spicy, sweet and moreish. I like them dripping with icing, and these, of course, include my other favourite ingredient – chocolate!

MAKES 11

Preparation time: 30 minutes, plus rising
Cooking time: 25–30 minutes

500ml (17fl oz) warm milk
150g (5oz) golden caster sugar
40g (1½oz) fresh yeast or 2 x (7g) sachets easy-bake dried yeast
200g (7oz) unsalted butter, melted, plus extra for greasing
2 tsp vanilla paste or extract
1 egg, plus 1 egg, beaten
1kg (2lb) plain flour, plus extra for dusting

For the filling
75g (3oz) dark chocolate, grated
100g (3½oz) unsalted butter, melted and cooled
200g (7oz) dark muscovado sugar
3 tbsp ground cinnamon

For the glaze
75g (3oz) golden icing sugar
1 tsp vanilla extract
1 tbsp water

Start by making the dough. Put the milk, sugar, yeast, melted butter, vanilla and whole egg into the bowl of a freestanding mixer fitted with a dough hook, then mix together until smooth. Sift the flour, then gradually add to the bowl, mixing until the dough comes away from the side of the bowl. Place the dough in a large, lightly floured bowl and cover with clingfilm or a damp tea towel. Leave to rise for 45 minutes–1 hour at room temperature, or until the dough has almost doubled in volume.

To make the filling, beat the grated chocolate, cooled melted butter, sugar and cinnamon in a bowl to a smooth, spreadable paste and put to one side.

When the dough has risen, knock it back to release the air, then turn out on to a lightly floured surface. Roll out the dough to an 8mm (½in) thick rectangle, about 28 x 70cm (11 x 27in). Using a palette knife, spread the filling all over the dough. Starting at a long edge, roll the dough into a long sausage shape without stretching it. Using a sharp knife, cut into slices about 6cm (2½in) wide. Place them on 2 greased and floured baking sheets. Cover with clingfilm or a damp tea towel and leave to rise for 30 minutes.

Preheat the oven to 200°C (fan 180°C)/400°F/gas mark 6. Meanwhile, add the water to the beaten egg to make an egg wash. Use a pastry brush and lightly brush the tops of the buns with the egg wash.

Bake the buns in the oven for 10 minutes, then reduce the heat to 180°C (fan 160°C)/350°F/gas mark 4 and cook for a further 15–20 minutes, or until golden brown, cooked in the centre and the buns sound hollow when tapped on the bases.

Meanwhile, to make the glaze, mix the icing sugar, vanilla and water together in a bowl. As soon as the buns are cooked, brush them generously with the glaze and leave to cool. These are fantastic served with coffee or hot chocolate.

DEVILISH CHOCOLATE BROWNIES

I know there are plenty of brownie recipes around, but this is my favourite dark chocolate version, and, of course, you can add nuts or dried fruits if you like. Remember, don't overcook them.

MAKES 16

Preparation time: 10 minutes
Cooking time: 30 minutes

200g (7oz) dark chocolate,
  roughly chopped
150g (5oz) unsalted butter,
  plus extra for greasing
2 tsp vanilla paste or extract
150g (5oz) golden caster sugar
3 eggs, beaten
75g (3oz) plain flour
2 tbsp cocoa powder
1 tsp salt
100g (3½oz) dark chocolate
  chips

Preheat the oven to 180°C (fan 160°C)/350°F/gas mark 4. Grease a 19cm (7½in) square shallow baking tin and line the base with baking paper.

Melt the chopped chocolate, butter and vanilla together in a heatproof bowl set over a saucepan of barely simmering water, making sure the surface of the water does not touch the bowl. Remove from the heat and stir in the sugar, then leave to cool for a few minutes.

Beat in the eggs, then sift in the flour, cocoa and salt and fold in until the mixture is smooth and glossy. Stir in the chocolate chips.

Pour the mixture into the prepared tin and level the top. Bake in the oven for 25 minutes, or until the top starts to crack but the centre remains gooey. Turn off the oven and leave the brownies inside for a further 5 minutes before removing. Leave to cool completely in the tin.

Cut the brownies into 16 small squares and remove from the tin. Store in an airtight container for up to 4 days.

MINI RED VELVET CAKES WITH WHITE CHOCOLATE FROSTING

This all-American favourite is now a worldwide sensation, and the use of oil and buttermilk make it extremely moist. My twist on the frosting makes this version even more indulgent.

MAKES 6

Preparation time: 40 minutes, plus cooling
Cooking time: 40 minutes

butter, for greasing
225g (7½oz) golden caster sugar
2 eggs
275 ml (9fl oz) vegetable oil
125ml (4fl oz) buttermilk
1 tbsp red food colouring
1 tsp vanilla extract
175g (6oz) plain flour
15g (½oz) cocoa powder
½ tsp baking powder
½ tsp salt
2 tsp white wine vinegar
icing sugar, for dusting

For the frosting
75g (3oz) white chocolate, roughly chopped
175g (6oz) unsalted butter, softened
375g (12oz) icing sugar
2 tbsp milk

Preheat the oven to 180°C (fan 160°C)/350°F/gas mark 4. Grease 7 x 6cm (2½in) diameter cooking rings 4cm (1½in) deep, line with baking paper, and place on a baking sheet lined with baking paper.

In a large bowl, whisk the eggs and sugar together using an electric hand whisk until pale. On slow speed, add the oil a little at a time until it has all been incorporated. Beat in the buttermilk, food colouring and vanilla. Sift the flour, cocoa powder, baking powder and salt together, then fold in, followed by the vinegar.

Divide the mixture between the cake rings, filling them three-quarters full. Bake in the oven for 35 minutes, or until a skewer inserted into the centres comes out clean.

Leave to cool in the rings for 5 minutes, then remove the cakes from the rings to a cooling rack to cool completely.

To make the frosting, melt the chocolate in a heatproof bowl set over a saucepan of barely simmering water, making sure the surface of the water does not touch the bowl. Leave to cool. Beat the butter and half the icing sugar together until smooth, then add the remaining icing sugar a little at a time, beating until the mixture is smooth. Add the milk and cooled chocolate and beat for a further 2 minutes.

To assemble, slice a mini cake horizontally into 3 layers. Thinly spread a layer of frosting on to the base layer, then sandwich the middle layer on top. Spread a little more frosting on the middle layer, then add the top layer. Repeat with 5 of the mini cakes so that you have 6 cakes in total leaving one spare. Spoon the remaining frosting into a piping bag fitted with a plain piping nozzle, then pipe around the edges of the cakes until completely covered. Crumble the remaining mini cake and sprinkle the crumbs over the tops of the piped cakes. Serve dusted with icing sugar.

FLOUR-FREE CHOCOLATE SPONGE

This is a great recipe, as the lack of flour makes this sponge really soft and moist and it is gluten free, too. It's so dark and chocolaty that I usually serve it with a little whipped cream and some fresh berries.

SERVES 6

Preparation time: 10 minutes
Cooking time: 40 minutes

125g (4oz) dark chocolate,
  roughly chopped
125g (4oz) unsalted butter,
  softened, plus extra for
  greasing
150g (5oz) golden caster sugar
3 eggs, beaten
1 tsp vanilla paste or extract
75g (3oz) cocoa powder

Preheat the oven to 170°C (fan 150°C)/325°F/gas mark 3. Grease a 20cm (8in) diameter, 6cm (2½ in) deep springform cake tin and line with baking paper.

Melt the chocolate in a heatproof bowl set over a saucepan of barely simmering water, making sure the surface of the water does not touch the bowl. Leave to cool.

In a large bowl, cream the butter and sugar together using an electric hand whisk until pale and fluffy. Beat in the eggs one at a time, followed by the cooled chocolate and the vanilla. Sift the cocoa powder and gently fold in.

Spoon the mixture into the prepared tin and bake in the oven for 35 minutes, or until a skewer inserted into the centre comes out clean. Leave to cool in the tin for 10 minutes, then turn out on to a cooling rack.

TIP

For an extra hit of cocoa, dust the inside of the greased tin with cocoa powder.

SOFT COOKIE DOUGH COOKIES

I simply adore these cookies. I love the soft centres, the rich flavour of the unrefined sugar and all the additions of nuts, chocolate chips or dried fruits, which make them so moreish and delicious.

MAKES 24

Preparation time: 15 minutes
Cooking time: 25–30 minutes

175g (6oz) unsalted butter, melted
200g (7oz) dark muscovado sugar
100g (3½oz) golden caster sugar
1 tsp vanilla extract or paste
2 eggs
250g (8oz) plain flour
½ tsp bicarbonate of soda
½ tsp salt
100g (3½oz) dark chocolate chips
100g (3½oz) white chocolate chips
100g (3½oz) macadamia nuts,
   roughly chopped

Preheat the oven to 180°C (fan 160°C)/350°F/gas mark 4. Line 2 baking sheets with baking paper.
....
In a large bowl, cream the melted butter, muscovado sugar and caster sugar together until smooth. Beat in the vanilla and eggs until light and creamy.
....
Sift the flour, bicarbonate of soda and salt together, then fold into the butter and sugar mixture until just combined. Stir in the chocolate chips and nuts.
....
Using an ice-cream scoop if possible, scoop the dough on to the prepared baking sheets, leaving at least 8cm (3½in) between each cookie, as they will spread in the oven. Do not flatten them before baking.
....
Bake in the oven for 12–15 minutes, or until the edges look golden brown but the centre is still soft. Leave to cool on the baking sheets for 5 minutes, then carefully transfer to a cooling rack to cool completely. Repeat with any remaining dough. Store the cookies in an airtight tin for up to a few days.

TIP
....
To vary the flavour, substitute the chocolate chips and macadamia nuts with dried fruits and different nuts.

DARK CHOCOLATE MOELLEUX

This extremely moist sponge is a perfect base for a celebration cake filled with a rich chocolate buttercream, coated with a glossy ganache and decorated with berries.

SERVES 12–14

Preparation time: 30 minutes,
  plus cooling and setting
Cooking time: 40–45 minutes

50g (2oz) dark chocolate,
  roughly chopped
350g (11½oz) butter, softened,
  plus extra for greasing
350g (11½oz) golden caster sugar
50g (2oz) black treacle
8 eggs, lightly beaten
300g (10oz) self-raising flour
50g (2oz) cocoa powder
2 tsp baking powder
50g (2oz) ground almonds
berries or dried fruits and nuts,
  to decorate
icing sugar, for dusting

For the ganache
200ml (7fl oz) whipping cream
200g (7oz) dark chocolate,
  chopped

For the buttercream
25g (1oz) dark chocolate,
  roughly chopped
200g (7oz) icing sugar, sifted
100g (3½ oz) unsalted butter,
  softened
a few drops of vanilla extract
2 tbsp double cream

First make the sponge. Preheat the oven to 170°C (fan 150°C)/325°F/gas mark 3. Grease 2 x 22cm (8½in) diameter sandwich cake tins and line with baking paper. Melt the chocolate in a heatproof bowl set over a saucepan of barely simmering water, making sure the surface of the water does not touch the bowl.

In a large bowl, cream the butter and sugar together until light and fluffy, then beat in the black treacle. Beat in the eggs a little at a time, then add the melted chocolate. Sift the flour, cocoa powder and baking powder together, then fold in with the ground almonds. Finish with an electric hand whisk to produce a smooth consistency.

Divide the mixture between the prepared tins and level the tops. Bake in the oven for 30–35 minutes, or until a skewer inserted into the centres comes out clean. Leave to cool in the tins, then turn out on to a cooling rack.

To make the ganache, put the whipping cream into a saucepan and heat to just below boiling point. Remove from the heat and add the chocolate, then use a wooden spoon to beat vigorously until melted and smooth. Leave to cool to room temperature.

To make the buttercream, melt the chocolate as above and leave to cool. In a bowl, cream the icing sugar and butter together using an electric hand whisk until light and fluffy. Beat in the vanilla, cooled chocolate and double cream to form a fairly stiff spreading consistency.

To assemble the cake, level the tops of the sponges using a sharp knife. Spread the buttercream over the top of one of the sponges and place it on a cooling rack set over a large plate or baking tray. Place the other sponge, upside down, on top to give a nice flat surface. Pour the ganache over the cake, completely covering it. Smooth with a palette knife and leave to set at room temperature. Serve decorated with berries or dried fruits and nuts, and lightly dusted with icing sugar.

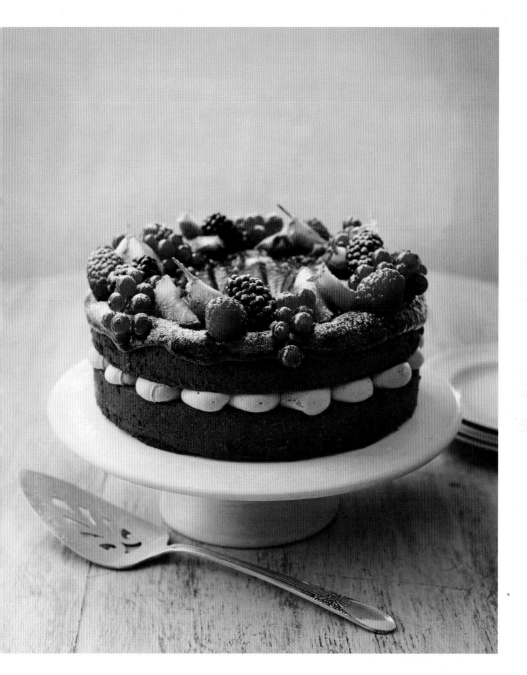

CHOCOLATE AND HAZELNUT MUFFINS

Most muffin recipes come as a fruity option for breakfast. These rich muffins are more a mid-afternoon treat especially if served warm straight from the oven.

MAKES 6

Preparation time: 15 minutes
Cooking time: 25–30 minutes

75g (3oz) dark chocolate, roughly chopped
50g (2oz) chocolate and hazelnut spread
175g (6oz) self-raising flour
½ tbsp baking powder
25g (1oz) cocoa powder
50g (2oz) golden caster sugar
2 eggs
1 tsp vanilla extract or paste
5 tbsp vegetable oil
4 tbsp milk
75g (3oz) dark chocolate chips
50g (2oz) chopped hazelnuts, roasted (see Tip on page 26)

Preheat the oven to 180°C (fan 160°C)/350°F/gas mark 4. Line a 6-hole deep muffin tin with paper muffin cases.

Gently melt the chocolate and chocolate spread together in a heatproof bowl set over a saucepan of barely simmering water, making sure the surface of the water does not touch the bowl. Leave to cool for a few minutes.

Sift the flour, baking powder and cocoa powder into a large bowl, then stir in the sugar. In a separate bowl, beat the eggs, vanilla, oil and milk together using an electric hand whisk. When combined, stir in the cooled chocolate. Fold the wet ingredients into the dry ingredients using a rubber spatula or metal spoon, but don't over-mix. Stir in the chocolate chips.

Divide the mixture between the muffin cases, filling them three-quarters full, then sprinkle the hazelnuts over the tops. Bake in the oven for 20–25 minutes, or until a skewer inserted into the centres comes out clean. When cooked, transfer to a cooling rack to cool.

TIP

This recipe will make 12 small cakes if you use a shallow bun tin.

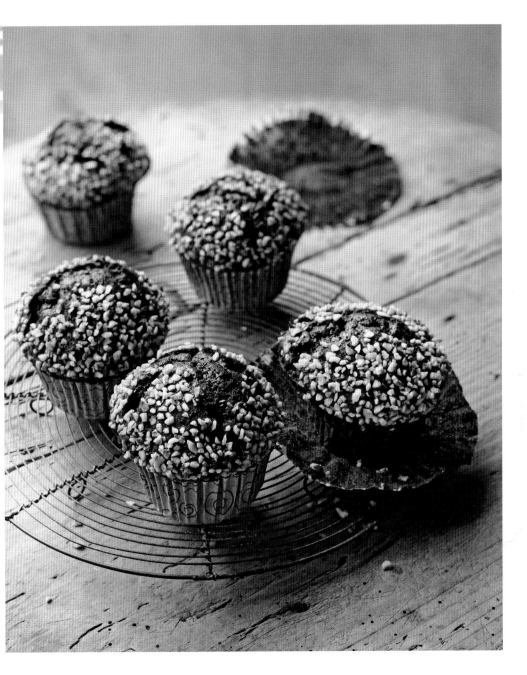

CHOCOLATE PAIN D'ÉPICE

Pain d'épice is a speciality from the east of France; this sticky loaf is usually served toasted with a spread of butter. This is my take on the traditional recipe, making it even more indulgent with chocolate.

SERVES 8

Preparation time: 15 minutes,
 plus overnight chilling
Cooking time: 50–55 minutes

butter, for greasing
200ml (7fl oz) milk
8 tbsp clear honey
125g (4oz) dark chocolate,
 finely chopped
300g (10oz) wholemeal flour
65g (2½oz) light muscovado
 sugar
1 tsp bicarbonate of soda
½ tsp ground cinnamon
½ tsp freshly grated nutmeg
½ tsp ground ginger
¼ tsp ground cloves
3 eggs, beaten
1 tbsp vanilla extract or paste
1 tbsp orange blossom water

Grease a 900g (2lb) loaf tin and line with baking paper.

Put the milk and honey into a small saucepan and heat gently but do not let it boil. Remove from the heat and add the chocolate, stirring until melted and blended together. Leave to cool for a few minutes.

Put the flour, sugar, bicarbonate of soda and spices into a large bowl and mix together. Make a well in the centre, then stir in the eggs, vanilla and orange blossom water, followed by the chocolate milk.

For best results, transfer the mixture to a food processor and blend for 2–3 minutes, or until smooth and very glossy. Alternatively, mix well using a wooden spoon. Pour the mixture into the prepared loaf tin, cover with clingfilm and leave to rest in the refrigerator overnight.

Bake the loaf in a preheated oven, 180°C (fan 160°C)/350°F/gas mark 4, for 45–50 minutes, or until a skewer inserted into the centre comes out clean. Leave to cool in the tin for 5 minutes, then transfer to a cooling rack to cool completely. The loaf keeps very well wrapped in clingfilm in an airtight container for up to 2 weeks.

TIP

Try toasting slices of this cake and spreading with butter or honey to serve.

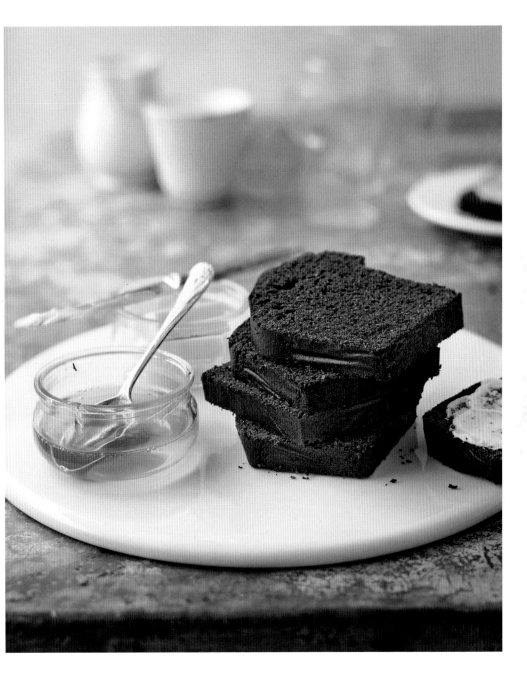

SWISS WALNUT AND CHOCOLATE CAKE

I used to make this recipe when I was a kid. I'm not too sure where the Swiss origin comes from, but even today it is still one of my all-time favourite cakes to make, as I love the combination of walnuts and chocolate.

SERVES 8

Preparation time: 15 minutes, plus cooling
Cooking time: 40–45 minutes

100g (3½oz) dark chocolate, roughly chopped
150g (5oz) unsalted butter, softened, plus extra for greasing
150g (5oz) golden caster sugar
2 eggs
75g (3oz) plain flour
2 tsp baking powder
2 tsp vanilla paste or extract
65g (2½oz) roasted and chopped walnuts (see Tip)
icing sugar, for dusting
50g walnut halves, to decorate

Preheat the oven to 180°C (fan 160°C)/350°F/gas mark 4. Grease a 22cm (8½in) diameter cake tin and line with baking paper.

Melt the chocolate in a heatproof bowl set over a saucepan of barely simmering water, making sure the surface of the water does not touch the bowl. Leave to cool for a few minutes.

In a large bowl, cream the butter and sugar together until pale and fluffy. Beat in the eggs one at the time. Sift the flour and baking powder together, then carefully fold in. Add the cooled chocolate and the vanilla, then fold in the chopped walnuts.

Spoon the mixture into the prepared tin. Arrange the extra walnut halves on top in a circular pattern and bake in the oven for 30–35 minutes, or until a skewer inserted into the centre comes out clean – the texture will be very similar to a brownie.

Leave to cool in the tin for 10 minutes, then remove from the tin and transfer to a cooling rack. Serve dusted with icing sugar. A hot crème anglaise is perfect as an accompaniment.

TIP

For roasted walnuts or any other nuts, simply spread whole nuts over a baking tray and roast in the oven at 180°C (fan 160°C)/350°F/gas mark 4 for 8–10 minutes, or until golden and crisp – be sure to watch them, as they can burn quickly. Leave to cool, then chop.

WHITE CHOCOLATE AND PEACH MELBA MUFFINS

These muffins are the perfect summer Sunday brunch as they are so delightfully fruity, fresh and yummy. My favourite and hopefully yours once tasted...

MAKES 12

Preparation time: 15 minutes
Cooking time: 25 minutes

300g (10oz) plain flour
2 tsp baking powder
1 egg
150g (5oz) golden caster sugar
1 tsp vanilla extract or paste
225ml (7½fl oz) milk
50g (2oz) unsalted butter, melted
and cooled
100g (3½oz) chopped peaches,
fresh or canned
125g (4oz) white chocolate,
cut into small chunks
100g (3½oz) fresh raspberries
icing sugar, for dusting

Preheat the oven to 180°C (fan 160°C)/350°F/gas mark 4. Line a 12-hole muffin tin with paper muffin cases.

Sift the flour and baking powder into a bowl. In a separate bowl, beat the egg and sugar together using an electric hand whisk, then whisk in the vanilla, milk and cooled melted butter. Using a rubber spatula or metal spoon, fold the wet ingredients into the dry ingredients until the mixture is smooth, but don't over-mix. Briefly fold in the peaches and white chocolate.

Divide the mixture between the muffin cases, filling them three-quarters full. Bake in the oven for 25 minutes, or until a skewer inserted into the centres comes out clean. Leave to cool on a cooling rack.

In a small bowl, roughly crush the raspberries with a fork. Spoon them on top of the muffins just before serving. Decorate with a dusting of icing sugar.

CHOCOLATE AND PISTACHIO BISCOTTI

Originally from Italy, biscotti now adorn coffee shops across the world – they are the perfect combination with good coffee. These chocolate and pistachio ones are to die for...

MAKES 26

Preparation time: 20 minutes, plus cooling
Cooking time: 50–55 minutes

100g (3½oz) unsalted butter, softened, plus extra for greasing
200g (7oz) golden caster sugar
2 eggs
275g (9oz) plain flour, plus extra for dusting
50g (2oz) cocoa powder
1 tsp bicarbonate of soda
125g (4oz) shelled pistachio nuts
75g (3oz) dark chocolate chips

Preheat the oven to 180°C (fan 160°C)/350°F/gas mark 4. Lightly grease 2 large baking sheets.

In a large bowl, cream the butter and sugar together until pale and fluffy. Beat in the eggs one at a time, then sift the flour, cocoa powder and bicarbonate of soda together and fold in. Gently stir in the pistachios and chocolate chips.

Turn the mixture out on to a floured surface and form into a large, slightly flattened loaf shape, about 30 x 7cm (12 x 3in). Carefully transfer to one of the prepared baking sheets and bake for 30 minutes. Remove from the oven and leave to cool for 10 minutes. Reduce the oven temperature to 150°C (fan 130°C)/300°F/gas mark 2.

Place the warm loaf on a chopping board and slice into 1cm (½in) thick slices. Arrange them on the baking sheets and return to the oven for a further 20–25 minutes, or until dry and crispy. Once cooked, transfer to a cooling rack to cool and harden.

You can store the biscotti in airtight containers for up to 2 weeks. They also make really nice presents when wrapped in a gift bag.

CHOCOLATE FLORENTINES

These little treats are great as a gift when boxed or bagged beautifully and they make a great accompaniment for after-dinner coffee.

MAKES 8

Preparation time: 20 minutes, plus cooling and setting
Cooking time: 8 minutes

50g (2oz) unsalted butter, softened, plus extra for greasing
50g (2oz) light muscovado sugar
2 tbsp plain flour
25g (1oz) toasted flaked almonds
25g (1oz) chopped hazelnuts, roasted (see Tip on page 26)
25g (1oz) chopped walnuts, roasted (see Tip on page 26)
50g (2oz) mixed peel
150g (5oz) milk chocolate, roughly chopped

Preheat the oven to 180°C (fan 160°C)/350°F/gas mark 4. Grease a baking sheet or 10cm (4in) silicone florentine moulds.

In a bowl, cream the butter and sugar together until pale and fluffy. Sift in the flour, then fold in all the nuts and the peel.

Place 8 heaped spoonfuls of the mixture on the prepared baking sheet, leaving enough space between each to expand, or fill the moulds. Bake in the oven for about 6–7 minutes, or until the florentines are golden. Leave to cool on the baking sheet or in the moulds until cold.

Melt the chocolate in a heatproof bowl set over a saucepan of barely simmering water, making sure the surface of the water does not touch the bowl. Using a pastry brush, coat the base of each florentine with the melted chocolate. Before the chocolate sets, create waves in the chocolate using a fork, then place, chocolate side up, on baking paper to set at room temperature. Store in a cool, dry place for up to 2 weeks.

TIP

To vary the flavours, replace the nuts with shelled pistachios, pine nuts or glacé cherries.

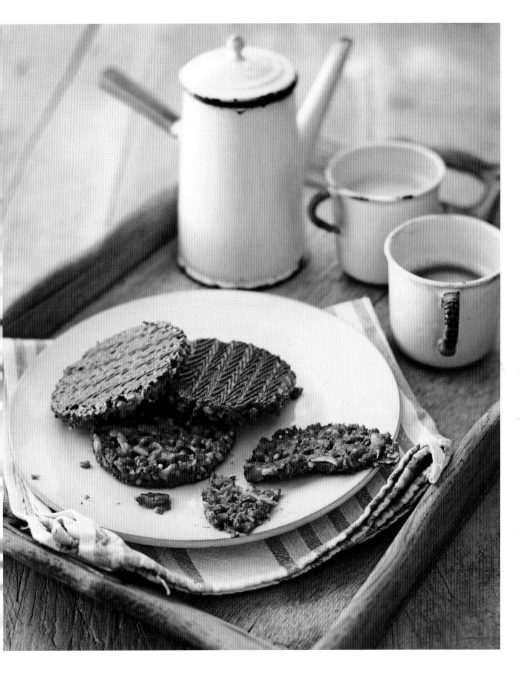

CHOCOLATE WAFFLES

As kids, we used to love going to Belgium for two reasons – first, the light, fluffy waffle, and second, the famous chocolate. This is my homage to these great trips – a combination of both waffle and chocolate.

MAKES 12–16

Preparation time: 5 minutes
Cooking time: 5 minutes per
  waffle

50g (2oz) cocoa powder
2 tsp ground cinnamon
250g (8oz) butter, melted
300g (10oz) golden caster sugar
4 eggs, beaten
250g (8oz) plain flour
2 tbsp milk
2 tsp vanilla paste or extract
icing sugar and cocoa powder,
  for dusting

Preheat a waffle iron. Sift the cocoa powder into a large bowl and stir in the cinnamon and melted butter. Add the sugar, eggs and flour, then whisk in the milk and vanilla until smooth.

Fill the waffle iron with some of the mixture and cook according to the manufacturer's instructions. Repeat until all the mixture is used.

Dust the waffles with icing sugar and cocoa powder and serve warm. These are great served with one of the chocolate sauces on pages 120–1.

BRETON SHORTBREAD WITH CHOCOLATE

Every pâtisserie or bakery in my birth region of Brittany will have this speciality in their display ... and each one will keep its recipe a secret! Here, I am sharing my grandmother Camille's recipe.

SERVES 8

Preparation time: 15 minutes
Cooking time: 40–45 minutes

350g (11½oz) plain flour
250g (8oz) golden caster sugar
250g (8oz) slightly salted butter,
   cubed, plus extra for greasing
6 egg yolks
2 tbsp dark rum
2 tsp vanilla extract
150g (5oz) dark chocolate chips

Preheat the oven to 180°C (fan 160°C)/350°F/gas mark 4. Grease a 24cm (9½in) diameter flan tin and line the base with baking paper.

Put the flour and sugar into a bowl and mix together. Add the butter and rub in using your fingertips until the mixture resembles fine breadcrumbs. In a separate bowl, beat 5 of the egg yolks with the rum and vanilla extract, then mix into the dry ingredients. Stir in the chocolate chips.

Spread the mixture into the prepared tin. Beat the remaining egg yolk, then brush over the top. Using a fork, make a crisscross design across the top.

Bake in the oven for 40–45 minutes, or until golden and cooked through. Leave to cool in the tin for a few minutes, then carefully turn out on to a cooling rack to cool completely.

CHOCOLATE SHORTBREADS

For over ten years I was a member of the beautiful Skibo Castle in Scotland. These chocolate shortbreads were always one of the highlights of the trip to this retreat.

MAKES 18

Preparation time: 15 minutes, plus chilling
Cooking time: 10–12 minutes

150g (5oz) slightly salted butter, softened, plus extra for greasing
125g (4oz) light muscovado sugar
2 tsp vanilla paste or extract
175g (6oz) plain flour
25g (1oz) cocoa powder
150g (5oz) dark chocolate chips
40g (1½oz) golden caster sugar

In a large bowl, cream the butter, muscovado sugar and vanilla together until pale and fluffy. Sift the flour and cocoa powder together, fold in and combine to form a crumbly dough. Stir in the chocolate chips.

Sprinkle the caster sugar on to a clean work surface. Form the dough into a 5cm (2in) diameter sausage, then roll in the sugar to coat. Cover with clingfilm and leave to rest in the refrigerator for at least 2 hours.

Preheat the oven to 180°C (fan 160°C)/350°F/gas mark 4. Grease 2 large baking sheets.

Using a large knife, cut the dough into 1cm (½in) thick discs and place on the prepared baking sheets. Bake in the oven for 10–12 minutes, or until the edges are firm to the touch. Leave to cool on the sheets, then store in an airtight tin or cookie jar for up to 1 week.

CHOCOLATE KOUGLOF

Alsace and the east of France are very famous for their baking and cooking. The Kouglof is a traditional recipe baked in a very characteristic-shaped mould. As well as looking good it tastes divine.

SERVES 8–10

Preparation time: 35 minutes, plus soaking and chilling overnight, and rising and cooling
Cooking time: 50–55 minutes

75g (3oz) golden sultanas
100ml (3½fl oz) Cognac
20g (¾oz) dried yeast
100g (3½oz) golden caster sugar
100ml (3½fl oz) lukewarm milk
500g (1lb) plain flour, plus extra for dusting
2 pinches of salt
3 eggs
200g (7oz) unsalted butter, cubed, plus extra for greasing
75g (3oz) almonds, chopped
2 tbsp mixed peel
100g (3½oz) dark chocolate chips

For the glaze
150g (5oz) dark chocolate, roughly chopped
50g (2oz) unsalted butter
2 tbsp icing sugar

Put the sultanas and brandy into a bowl and leave to soak overnight at room temperature.

The following day, put the yeast, sugar and milk in a separate bowl and mix gently to dissolve. Leave to stand for 10 minutes.

Sift the flour and salt into the bowl of a freestanding mixer fitted with a dough hook. Add the eggs and yeast mixture and mix together for 10 minutes, or until the dough comes away from the side of the bowl. Add the butter a little at a time until well incorporated. Add the remaining ingredients, including the soaked sultanas, and mix for a further 5 minutes.

Grease and flour a 2 litre (3½ pint) kouglof mould. Push the dough into it, cover with clingfilm and chill in the refrigerator overnight. The following day, remove the mould from the refrigerator and leave the dough to rise for 4–5 hours at room temperature.

Bake the kouglof in a preheated oven, 170°C (fan 150°C)/325°F/ gas mark 3, for 45–50 minutes, or until golden. Turn out of the mould on to a cooling rack and leave to cool completely.

To make the glaze, melt the chocolate and butter together in a heatproof bowl set over a saucepan of barely simmering water, making sure the surface of the water does not touch the bowl. When melted, fold in the sugar. Pour the glaze over the top of the cake and leave to set. Traditionally, this cake is served with beaten crème fraîche.

CHOCOLATE, PUMPKIN AND PECAN CAKE

I'd describe this cake as a perfect winter warmer, full of very earthy flavours and a spicy, nutty crunch. It's best eaten a day after baking.

SERVES 8

Preparation time: 20 minutes, plus cooling and resting overnight
Cooking time: 1 hour 25 minutes

125g (4oz) pecan nuts
1 tsp cayenne pepper
225g (7½oz) dark chocolate, roughly chopped
150g (5oz) unsalted butter, plus extra for greasing 3 eggs
275g (9oz) dark muscovado sugar
275ml (9fl oz) water
3 tsp vanilla paste or extract
250g (8oz) self-raising flour
3 tsp ground cinnamon
100g (3½oz) peeled, deseeded pumpkin, grated
cocoa powder, for dusting

Preheat the oven to 170°C (fan 150°C)/325°F/gas mark 3. Grease a 23cm (9in) diameter springform cake tin and line with baking paper.

In a large bowl, mix the pecans and cayenne pepper together. Place the nuts on a baking sheet and roast in the oven for 10 minutes, or until they are golden and crunchy. Leave to cool, then roughly chop.

Melt the chocolate and butter together in a heatproof bowl set over a saucepan of barely simmering water, making sure the surface of the water does not touch the bowl.

Beat the eggs and sugar together in a bowl until nice and smooth, then beat in the melted chocolate mixture, followed by the water and vanilla. Sift the flour and cinnamon together, then fold in until smooth. Fold in the pumpkin and chopped pecans.

Spoon the mixture into the prepared tin and bake in the oven for 1 hour 10 minutes, or until a skewer inserted into the centre comes out clean. Leave to cool in the tin for 10 minutes, then turn out on to a cooling rack to cool completely.

Wrap the cake in clingfilm and store at room temperature for at least 24 hours before eating. Dust with cocoa powder before serving.

DESSERTS
AND PUDDINGS

APRICOT AND CHOCOLATE CHARLOTTE

This was my mum's favourite recipe. She used to make this spectacular dessert on Sunday when we had guests. It has to be made the day before, which makes your life easier on the day if you are entertaining.

SERVES 6

Preparation time: 30 minutes, plus cooling and chilling overnight
Cooking time: 15 minutes

butter, for greasing
30–35 sponge finger biscuits

For the apricots
50ml (2fl oz) water
100g (3½oz) golden caster sugar
300g (10oz) fresh apricots, stoned and diced
juice of 1 lemon
5g (¼oz) unsalted butter
2 tsp clear honey
1 tbsp apricot preserve
2 tsp balsamic vinegar

For the chocolate mousse
100g (3½oz) dark chocolate, roughly chopped
25g (1oz) unsalted butter
3 tbsp crème fraîche
2 egg yolks
100g (3½oz) egg whites
15g (½oz) golden caster sugar

Start with the apricots. Put the water and sugar into a saucepan and heat gently until the sugar has dissolved. Put the apricots into a heatproof bowl, then pour over the syrup and add the lemon juice. Leave to cool, then drain the apricots, reserving the syrup.

Melt the butter in a small frying pan. Add the apricots and fry until golden. Remove from the heat and add the honey, apricot preserve and vinegar. Return to the heat and cook for a further 2 minutes, then leave to cool.

For the chocolate mousse, melt the chocolate and butter together in a heatproof bowl set over a saucepan of barely simmering water, making sure the surface of the water does not touch the bowl. Remove from the heat and fold in the crème fraîche first, then the egg yolks. In a clean, dry bowl, whisk the egg whites and sugar to stiff peaks, then gently fold into the chocolate mixture to form a lovely smooth mousse.

To make the charlotte, lightly grease a 15cm (6in) diameter charlotte mould and line the base with baking paper. Dip the sponge fingers into the reserved apricot syrup, then use to carefully line the charlotte mould, making sure they are tightly placed.

Spoon one-third of the chocolate mousse over the base, spoon over half of the cooled apricots, then cover with a layer of dipped sponge fingers. Repeat the layers, finishing with a layer of sponge fingers. If necessary, trim off any excess sponge from around the edge to level the top. Cover the top with greaseproof paper and place a few small plates on top as weights. Leave to chill in the refrigerator overnight.

One hour before serving, turn the charlotte out on to a serving plate and leave to stand at room temperature. Decorate with any leftover apricots and serve with crème fraîche.

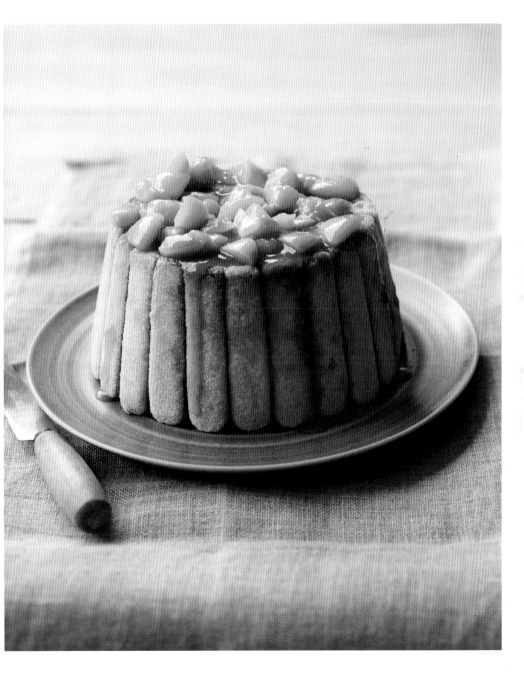

CHOCOLATE PETITS POTS

If you like a small treat at the end of a meal, this recipe is for you. It's a classic you will find in most French bistros and because of its size it won't make you feel too guilty.

SERVES 8

Preparation time: 10 minutes,
  plus cooling and chilling
Cooking time: 5 minutes

1 litre (1¾ pints) milk
200g (7oz) dark chocolate,
  roughly chopped
50g (2oz) light muscovado sugar
75g (3oz) cornflour
50g (2oz) unsalted butter,
  cut into small cubes
2 tsp brandy

Reserve 150ml (¼ pint) of the milk and pour the remainder into a small saucepan. Add the chocolate and sugar and heat gently, stirring until the sugar has completely dissolved.

Blend the cornflour with the reserved milk in a bowl using a small balloon whisk, then stir into the chocolate milk and bring to the boil, stirring continuously. Remove from the heat and add the butter, then stir in the brandy.

Pour into 8 small cups or ramekin dishes. Leave to cool, then leave to set in the refrigerator for at least 4 hours. Remove from the refrigerator 1 hour before serving.

TIP

To vary the flavour, substitute the brandy with orange liqueur, kirsch, cassis or framboise.

CHOCOLATE AND TONKA BEAN CRÈME BRÛLÉES

Tonka beans are sweet and deliciously perfumed with vanilla and rich milk chocolate. This strong spice adds a touch of suave luxury to the brûlées.

SERVES 6

Preparation time: 15 minutes, plus chilling overnight
Cooking time: 1 hour 10 minutes

100g (3½oz) dark chocolate, finely chopped
1 tonka bean
600ml (1 pint) double cream
8 egg yolks
75g (3oz) golden caster sugar
4 tbsp demerara sugar

Preheat the oven to 110°C (fan 90°C)/225°F/gas mark ¼. Place 6 brûlée dishes or flameproof ramekins into a shallow roasting tin and fill the tin with water to come halfway up the sides of the dishes.

Put the chocolate into a heatproof bowl. Using a nutmeg grater, grate the tonka bean, then mix with the chocolate. Put the cream into a saucepan and heat to just below boiling point, then pour over the chocolate and mix gently until the chocolate has melted.

In a separate bowl, whisk the egg yolks and caster sugar together using an electric hand whisk until pale and fluffy. Whisk the chocolate cream a little at a time into the egg mixture.

Pour into the dishes in the bain-marie and bake in the oven for 1 hour, or until set.

Leave to cool, then chill in the refrigerator overnight.

To serve, sprinkle demerara sugar over the top of each crème, then caramelize using a kitchen blowtorch.

TIP

If you do not have a kitchen blowtorch, sprinkle the crème brûlées with the sugar and put on a baking sheet. Place under a hot grill until the sugar caramelizes.

RASPBERRY AND CHOCOLATE TART

As well as the great combination of dark chocolate and raspberries, the addition of the chocolate shortcrust pastry gives a three-dimensional taste and texture to this yummy recipe.

SERVES 6

Preparation time: 25 minutes, plus chilling and cooling
Cooking time: 25 minutes

175g (6oz) plain flour, plus extra for dusting
50g (2oz) cocoa powder
50g (2oz) golden icing sugar
150g (5oz) unsalted butter, cubed, plus extra for greasing
3 egg yolks
1 tsp vanilla extract
500g (1lb) raspberries
icing sugar, for dusting

For the ganache
200g (7oz) dark chocolate, roughly chopped
200ml (7fl oz) single cream
2 tsp vanilla extract
75g (3oz) unsalted butter

Sift the flour, cocoa powder and icing sugar together into a large bowl. Add the butter and rub in using your fingertips until the mixture resembles fine breadcrumbs. Add the egg yolks and gently mix together, then add the vanilla and combine to form a smooth dough. Cover with clingfilm and leave to rest in the refrigerator for at least 30 minutes.

Preheat the oven to 190°C (fan 170°C)/375°F/gas mark 5. Lightly grease a 24cm (9½in) diameter tart tin.

Roll out the pastry on a lightly floured surface and carefully use to line the tin. Cover with ovenproof clingfilm and prick a few holes to avoid pockets of air while it bakes. Fill the pastry case with baking beans and bake in the oven for 15 minutes. Remove the clingfilm and beans and return to the oven for a further 5 minutes. Leave to cool.

To make the ganache, melt the chocolate in a heatproof bowl set over a saucepan of barely simmering water, making sure the surface of the water does not touch the bowl. Meanwhile, put the cream into a saucepan and heat until steaming hot, but do not let it boil. Remove the melted chocolate from the heat and slowly pour in the cream, gently stirring. Add the vanilla, then the butter and stir together.

Pack the cooled pastry case with raspberries, saving a few for decoration. Pour the hot chocolate ganache over the raspberries to fill to the top of the pastry. Leave to set in the refrigerator for at least 30 minutes. Serve decorated with the reserved raspberries dusted with a little icing sugar.

PEAR AND CHOCOLATE CLAFOUTIS

Clafoutis is a very rustic dish usually made with cherries. This dessert has had a bit of a revival and you will love this combination. I make it with raw pears to give a nice crunch.

SERVES 6

Preparation time: 20 minutes, plus chilling
Cooking time: 25–30 minutes

unsalted butter, for greasing
1 tbsp muscovado sugar
250g (8oz) dark chocolate, roughly chopped
50g (2oz) plain flour
1 tsp ground cinnamon
4 eggs
50ml (2fl oz) whipping cream
200ml (7fl oz) milk
4 ripe pears, peeled, cored and thickly sliced

Preheat the oven to 180°C (fan 160°C)/350°F/gas mark 4. Grease a 1.5 litre (2½ pint) ceramic gratin dish and sprinkle with the sugar.

Melt the chocolate in a heatproof bowl set over a saucepan of barely simmering water, making sure the surface of the water does not touch the bowl.

Sift the flour and cinnamon together into a bowl, then beat in the eggs, cream and milk to form a batter. Stir in the melted chocolate, then pour it into the prepared dish. Sprinkle the pears all over the chocolate custard, letting them sink.

Bake in the oven for 20–25 minutes, or until set. Leave to cool completely in the dish, then chill in the refrigerator before serving.

HOT CHOCOLATE SOUFFLÉS

I love soufflé. It is such a simple recipe with few ingredients, but it still has the wow factor every time you make one. This chocolate version, especially when served with a vanilla ice-cream drop, is superb.

SERVES 6

Preparation time: 20 minutes
Cooking time: 15 minutes

unsalted butter, for greasing
125g (4oz) dark chocolate,
　roughly chopped
2 tsp dark rum (optional)
2 tbsp crème fraîche
4 eggs, separated, plus 2 egg
　whites
pinch of salt
icing sugar, for dusting

Preheat the oven to 200°C (fan 180°C)/400°F/gas mark 6. Grease 6 ramekin dishes.

Melt the chocolate in a heatproof bowl set over a saucepan of barely simmering water, making sure the surface of the water does not touch the bowl. Stir in the rum, if using. Remove from the heat and add the crème fraîche, then the egg yolks.

In a large, clean, dry bowl, whisk all the egg whites and the salt to soft peaks.

Fold one-quarter of the egg whites into the chocolate mixture, then fold in the remaining whites.

Fill the prepared ramekins to the top with the mixture, then clean the rims using your finger and thumb. Place on a baking sheet and bake in the oven for 10–12 minutes, or until nicely risen. Dust with icing sugar and serve immediately.

TIP

For a delicious party trick, serve your soufflés with an ice-cream drop. Before you make the soufflés, scoop out 6 balls of good-quality vanilla ice cream and place on a freezer-proof plate. Keep in the freezer until ready to serve. When serving the soufflés at the table, drop an ice-cream ball into each soufflé.

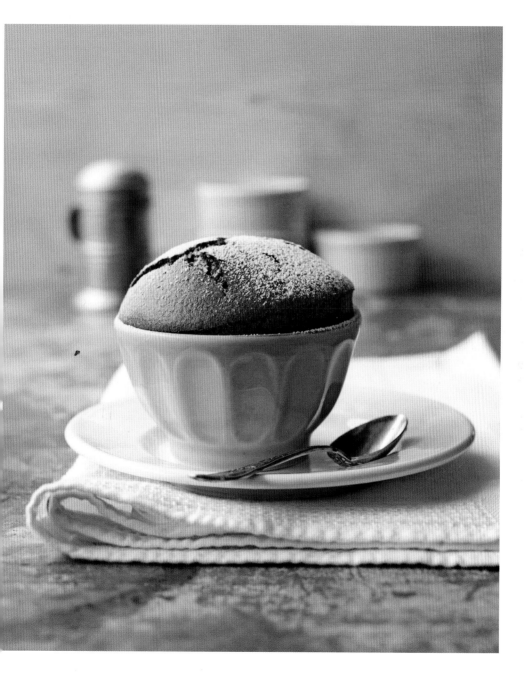

CHOCOLATE AND BANANA TARTE TATIN

This is a great winter dessert and seriously indulgent. The chocolate, caramel-infused bananas are full of flavour and the delicate pastry simply melts in your mouth.

SERVES 6

Preparation time: 15 minutes
Cooking time: 30–35 minutes

350g (11½oz) ready-made all-butter puff pastry
plain flour, for dusting
100g (3½oz) light muscovado sugar
50g (2oz) unsalted butter, plus extra for greasing
75g (3oz) dark chocolate, finely chopped
2 cinnamon sticks
5 firm bananas, cut into large chunks

Preheat the oven to 200°C (fan 180°C)/400°F/gas mark 6. Grease a 22cm (8½in) diameter tarte tatin tin. Roll out the pastry on a floured surface to a disc 2.5cm (1in) larger than the tin. Put to one side.

Put the sugar and butter into the tin and cook gently over a medium heat until it forms a dark blond caramel. Remove from the heat and add the chocolate, stirring until melted. Drop the cinnamon sticks into the centre of the tin.

Arrange the banana chunks tightly in the tin. Place the pastry over the top, tucking in the overhanging pastry between the fruit and the tin. Using a small knife, pierce the top of the pastry to allow the steam to escape.

Bake in the oven for 25–30 minutes, or until the pastry is puffed up and golden. Invert on to a serving dish immediately. Serve with crème fraîche or ice cream.

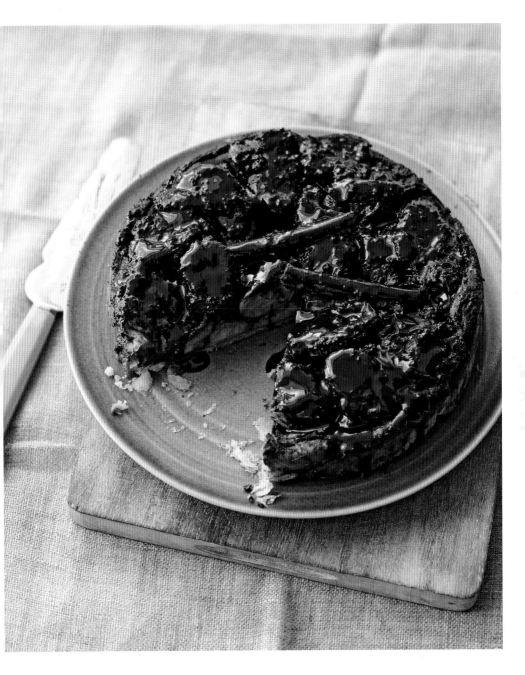

CHOCOLATE AND CHESTNUT TRUFFLE CAKES

One of my favourite areas of France is Lozère, a mountain region with a great food legacy. Chestnuts are very popular in both cooking and baking, and are used to make chestnut flour, which is gluten free. The flavour of chestnuts works very well with chocolate.

SERVES 6

Preparation time: 15 minutes
Cooking time: 25 minutes

125g (4oz) dark chocolate,
  roughly chopped
125g (4oz) unsalted butter,
  plus extra for greasing
300g (10oz) sweetened chestnut
  paste
1 tsp vanilla paste or extract
2 tbsp chestnut flour
4 eggs, separated
chopped glacé chestnuts,
  to decorate

Preheat the oven to 180°C (fan 160°C)/350°F/gas mark 4. Grease 6 x individual 10cm (4in) diameter loose-bottomed tart tins and line the bases with baking paper.

Gently melt the chocolate and butter together in a heatproof bowl set over a saucepan of barely simmering water, making sure the surface of the water does not touch the bowl.

Remove from the heat and stir in the chestnut paste and vanilla. Add the flour, then beat in the egg yolks one at a time. In a clean, dry bowl, whisk the egg whites to soft peaks, then fold into the chestnut mixture.

Divide the mixture between the prepared tins, filling them three-quarters full. Bake in the oven for 18–20 minutes, or until a skewer inserted into the centres comes out clean. Leave to cool in the tins for 5 minutes, then remove and transfer on to serving plates. Serve warm, topped with glacé chestnuts to decorate, drizzle with honey, along with a jug of pouring cream.

TIP

Sweetened chestnut paste or spread (crème de marrons) is available canned from good delicatessens and some larger supermarkets.

CHOCOLATE OMELETTE SOUFFLÉ

Not far from where I grew up in France there is a restaurant, at Mont Saint-Michel, famous for its sweet omelette soufflé. This is my take on Madame Poulard's secret recipe.

SERVES 1

Preparation time: 10 minutes
Cooking time: 10 minutes

200g (7oz) fresh mixed red
  berries
2 tsp berry preserve
25g (1oz) dark chocolate,
  roughly chopped
1 egg yolk
1½ tbsp golden caster sugar,
  plus an extra 2 tsp
1 tsp vanilla paste or extract
2 egg whites
10g (½oz) unsalted butter
icing sugar, for dusting

Put the berries and berry preserve into a saucepan and cook over a medium heat for 1 minute, or until the berries start to puff up. Remove from the heat and put to one side.

Melt the chocolate in a heatproof bowl set over a saucepan of barely simmering water, making sure the surface of the water does not touch the bowl.

Put the egg yolk, the 2 teaspoons of caster sugar and vanilla into a bowl and mix together, then stir in the chocolate.

In a clean, dry bowl, whisk the egg whites to stiff peaks, adding the remaining caster sugar a little at a time. Fold one-quarter of the egg whites into the chocolate to loosen the mixture, then fold in the remaining whites.

Melt the butter in a small 16cm (6½in) diameter flameproof nonstick frying pan over a medium heat, and meanwhile preheat the grill to a medium-high heat. Spoon the chocolate mixture into the pan, making sure it is an even layer, and cook for 2–3 minutes, then place under the grill for 1 minute, or until set, making sure it does not burn.

Spoon the berry mixture over one half of the omelette. Fold the omelette over to enclose the filling, then dust with icing sugar. Serve immediately.

TIP

Use egg whites at room temperature to get the most volume when whisking.

WHITE CHOCOLATE
AND PASSION FRUIT CHEESECAKE

I am a big fan of the baked cheesecake and this recipe is smooth and zesty with a touch
of the exotic. It's perfectly sweetened with the white chocolate – a great summer dessert.

SERVES 6

Preparation time: 30 minutes,
plus cooling and chilling
overnight
Cooking time: 1 hour 5 minutes–
1 hour 15 minutes

100g (3½oz) digestive biscuits,
crushed
50g (2oz) unsalted butter, melted,
plus extra for greasing
125g (4oz) white chocolate,
chopped
125ml (4fl oz) single cream
225g (7½oz) cream cheese,
softened
225g (7½oz) mascarpone cheese
4 tbsp golden caster sugar
2 tsp vanilla extract
4 eggs, separated
125ml (4fl oz) passion fruit pulp,
sieved to remove the pips
passion fruit, to decorate

Preheat the oven to 180°C (fan 160°C)/350°F/gas mark 4.
Grease a 20cm (8in) diameter springform cake tin.

Put the crushed biscuits and melted butter into a bowl and mix well.
Tip the mixture into the prepared tin and press down with the back
of a spoon. Bake in the oven for 10 minutes, or until golden. Leave
to cool. Reduce the oven temperature to 150°C (fan 130°C)/300°F/
gas mark 2.

Put the chocolate into a heatproof bowl. Put the cream into a small
saucepan and heat until steaming hot, but do not let it boil. Pour the
cream on to the chocolate and stir until smooth. Put to one side.

In a separate bowl, beat the cream cheese and mascarpone together
until smooth. Add the sugar, vanilla and egg yolks. Stir in the white
chocolate mixture and passion fruit pulp.

In a large, clean, dry bowl, whisk 2 egg whites to soft peaks (save
the remaining 2 egg whites for another recipe). Fold a large spoonful
of the egg whites into the batter vigorously to loosen the mixture,
then gently fold in the remaining whites until smooth.

Spoon the mixture on to the cooled base and bake for 50–60 minutes,
or until set but with a slight wobble in the centre. Turn off the oven
and leave the cheesecake to cool inside for 2 hours, with the door
ajar. Chill in the refrigerator overnight.

Remove from the tin and decorate with fresh passion fruit quarters.

CHOCOLATE COFFEE BAKED CHEESECAKE

Cheesecakes are always popular and I have to say I am a great fan of a baked cheesecake. The chocolate in this recipe is enhanced by the addition of the rich, strong coffee flavour.

SERVES 6–8

Preparation time: 30 minutes,
   plus chilling and cooling
Cooking time: 1 hour 35 minutes

175g (6oz) chocolate cookies,
   crushed
50g (2oz) unsalted butter, melted,
   plus extra for greasing
250g (8oz) cream cheese
250g (8oz) mascarpone cheese
100g (3½oz) golden caster sugar
150ml (¼ pint) double cream
1 tsp vanilla paste or extract
1 tbsp plain flour
2 eggs, plus 1 egg yolk
1 tsp instant coffee
2 tsp hot water
2 tsp coffee extract
pure cocoa powder, for dusting

For the chocolate topping
15g (½oz) unsalted butter
1 tbsp crème fraîche
50g (2oz) light muscovado sugar
150g (5oz) dark chocolate, finely
   chopped
1 tsp coffee extract

Preheat the oven to 150°C (fan 130°C)/300°F/gas mark 2. Grease a 22cm (8½in) diameter springform cake tin.

Put the crushed cookies and melted butter into a bowl and mix well. Tip the mixture into the prepared tin and press down with the back of a spoon. Leave to set in the refrigerator for 15 minutes.

Put the cream cheese, mascarpone, sugar, cream, vanilla and flour into a large bowl and beat together until nice and smooth. Beat in the eggs and egg yolk. Dissolve the coffee in the hot water, then beat into the mixture with the coffee extract.

Spoon the mixture on to the chilled base and bake in the oven for 1 hour 30 minutes, or until set but still with a slight wobble in the centre. Turn off the oven and leave the cheesecake to cool inside for 2 hours, with the door ajar. Chill in the refrigerator.

To make the chocolate topping, put the butter, crème fraîche and sugar into a small saucepan and heat gently until melted. Add the chocolate and coffee extract and heat gently for a further 2 minutes, stirring continuously. Remove from the heat, then give the mixture a good whisk. Leave to cool for a few minutes, then pour over the chilled cheesecake. Return to the refrigerator and leave to set.

Remove from the tin and dust generously with cocoa powder. Serve with whipped vanilla cream.

ICED BERRIES WITH WHITE CHOCOLATE SAUCE

Inspired by a birthday meal at The Ivy restaurant in London, this is a really delicious last-minute solution and a refreshing summer dessert.

SERVES 6

Preparation time: 10 minutes, plus chilling
Cooking time: 5 minutes

500g (1lb) mixed frozen berries
150ml (¼ pint) double cream
150g (5oz) white chocolate, roughly chopped
1 tsp vanilla extract
2 tbsp white rum (optional)

Put the frozen berries into the refrigerator 1 hour before serving so that they soften but are still icy.

To make the sauce, put the cream, chocolate and vanilla into a small saucepan and heat gently, stirring continuously, until the chocolate has melted. Leave to cool for 2 minutes, then stir in the rum, if using.

Divide the berries between 6 shallow bowls and pour over the hot sauce. Serve immediately before the fruits completely defrost.

TIP

Use a mixture of blackberries, blueberries, raspberries and redcurrants for a perfect summer dessert.

FRENCH BISTRO CHOCOLATE MOUSSE

One of my favourite bistros in Paris is called Chez Janou. Apart from the great atmosphere, the best thing there is the chocolate mousse made the old-fashioned way and served in a large pottery vat with a ladle – and you can eat as much as you want. A dream!

SERVES 6

Preparation time: 15 minutes, plus chilling
Cooking time: 5 minutes

250g (8oz) dark chocolate, roughly chopped
65g (2½oz) unsalted butter
6 eggs, separated
pinch of salt

Melt the chocolate and butter together in a heatproof bowl set over a saucepan of barely simmering water, making sure the surface of the water does not touch the bowl. Remove from the heat, then beat in the egg yolks.

In a large, clean, dry bowl, whisk the egg whites and salt to stiff peaks. Fold a large spoonful of the egg whites into the chocolate mixture to loosen, then gently fold in the remaining whites.

Pour the mixture into a serving dish, cover with clingfilm and chill in the refrigerator for at least 4 hours. The mousse is lovely served with Breton Shortbread with Chocolate (see page 34).

TIP

For a grown-up version, add a little orange liqueur, amaretto liqueur or Cognac to the mixture.

CHOCOLATE 'SAMOSAS'

These unusually sweet samosas are great for a party to serve as a canapé, or even as a dessert with some exotic ice cream, such as mango ice cream.

MAKES 4

Preparation time: 10 minutes
Cooking time: 10 minutes

25g (1oz) unsalted butter
2 ripe bananas, sliced
1 tbsp light muscovado sugar
2 sheets of brik or filo pastry
50g (2oz) dark chocolate,
    finely grated
½ tsp ground cinnamon

Melt half the butter in a frying pan, add the banana slices and sugar and fry for about 4–5 minutes, or until the bananas have caramelized, turning them over halfway during cooking.

Cut the pastry sheets in half. Place banana slices and a good sprinkling of chocolate and cinnamon towards one end of each pastry sheet, then fold up to resemble a triangular 'samosa' shape.

Heat the remaining butter in the frying pan over a medium heat, add the pastries and cook for about 2 minutes each side, or until golden brown all over. Serve immediately.

CHOCOLATE AND FRAMBOISE ROULADE

This recipe is inspired by my mentors Albert and Michel Roux's classic recipe Le Roule Marquis, which I used to bake when working for them. This recipe is very light and contains no flour.

SERVES 10

Preparation time: 35 minutes, plus cooling and chilling
Cooking time: 25 minutes

50g caster sugar
50ml (2fl oz) water
25ml (1fl oz) crème de framboise
50g (2oz) icing sugar
300ml (10fl oz) double cream, whipped to soft peaks
500g (1lb) fresh raspberries, plus extra to decorate

For the sponge
butter, for greasing
175g (6oz) dark chocolate, roughly chopped
6 eggs, separated
175g (6oz) caster sugar
1 tsp vanilla paste
2 tbsp cocoa powder, sifted

First make the sponge. Preheat the oven to 180°C (fan 160°C)/350°F/gas mark 4. Lightly grease a 38cm x 28cm (15 x 11in) baking tray and line with baking paper.

Melt the chocolate in a heatproof bowl set over a saucepan of barely simmering water, making sure the surface of the water does not touch the bowl. Leave to cool for a few minutes.

In a large bowl, whisk the sugar and egg yolks together using an electric hand whisk until pale and creamy. Add the vanilla paste and cooled chocolate and stir until smooth. In a large, clean, dry bowl, whisk the egg whites to stiff peaks. Fold the egg whites into the chocolate mixture, then fold in the cocoa powder.

Spoon the mixture into the prepared tray and gently level the top using a palette knife. Bake in the oven for 18–20 minutes, or until firm to the touch. Place a sheet of nonstick baking paper on top of the sponge, then put a clean, damp tea towel on top of the paper. Leave to cool.

Meanwhile, make a syrup by putting the caster sugar and water into a small saucepan and heating gently until the sugar has dissolved. Boil for 2 minutes, then turn off the heat and leave to cool completely before stirring in the framboise.

To assemble, dust a large piece of nonstick baking paper with some of the icing sugar, then turn the roulade out on to it and peel off the lining paper. Brush the framboise syrup over the sponge, then spread over the whipped cream and cover with raspberries.

Start from a long edge and roll up the sponge tightly to start with and use the paper to help you. The roulade may crack when you do this, but that's part of its charm! Chill in the refrigerator for at least 4 hours. To serve, dust generously with the remaining icing sugar and serve with extra raspberries.

MILK, DARK AND WHITE CHOCOLATE VERRINES

Serving desserts in small shot glasses is now very popular, especially for parties and functions. This trio of chocolate looks great and, of course, tastes great, too.

SERVES 8 OR FILLS 20 SHOT GLASSES

Preparation time: 35 minutes, plus chilling
Cooking time: 25 minutes

For the dark chocolate layer
75g (3oz) dark chocolate, roughly chopped
1 tbsp golden caster sugar
2 eggs, separated

For the milk chocolate layer
75g (3oz) milk chocolate, roughly chopped
½ tbsp golden caster sugar
2 eggs, separated

For the white chocolate layer
2 egg yolks
2 tsp golden caster sugar
1 tsp cold water
150g (5oz) white chocolate, roughly chopped
250ml (8fl oz) double cream

Start with the dark chocolate layer. Melt the chocolate and sugar together in a heatproof bowl set over a saucepan of barely simmering water, making sure the surface of the water does not touch the bowl. Remove from the heat and stir in the egg yolks. In a clean, dry bowl, whisk the egg whites to firm peaks, then fold into the chocolate mixture. Divide the mixture evenly between glasses or shot glasses. Leave to set in the refrigerator.

Next, make the milk chocolate layer as above. Carefully pour it over the set layer in the glasses and return to the refrigerator to set.

Finally, make the white chocolate layer. Put the egg yolks, sugar and water into a heatproof bowl and mix together. Set the bowl over a saucepan of simmering water and whisk for 10 minutes using an electric hand whisk. Remove from the heat and continue to whisk until the mixture is thick and creamy.

Melt the white chocolate in separate heatproof bowl set over the simmering water, then leave to cool for a few minutes. Lightly whip the cream to soft peaks. Stir the cooled chocolate into the egg mixture, then fold in the whipped cream. Carefully pour the mixture over the set layer in the glasses and chill in the refrigerator for at least 6 hours until completely set. Serve decorated with grated chocolate.

WHITE CHOCOLATE, RASPBERRY AND LEMON BATTENBERG

This is my take on a great British cake, making it lighter, colourful and a touch more contemporary in presentation, too.

SERVES 8

Preparation time: 45 minutes, plus cooling
Cooking time: 30–35 minutes

350g (11½oz) unsalted butter, softened, plus extra for greasing
350g (11½oz) golden caster sugar

275g (9oz) self-raising flour
100g (3½oz) ground almonds
1 tsp baking powder
6 eggs
1 tsp vanilla paste or extract
2 tbsp milk
2 tbsp freeze-dried raspberry pieces
2 tsp raspberry extract
few drops of pink food colouring
2 tsp lemon extract
few drops of yellow food colouring
150g (5oz) raspberry preserve
icing sugar, for dusting
300g (10oz) white modelling chocolate
fresh raspberries, to decorate

Preheat the oven to 180°C (fan 160°C)/350°F/gas mark 4. Grease 2 x 20cm (8in) square cake tins or a Battenberg tin and line with baking paper.

Put the butter, caster sugar, flour, ground almonds, baking powder, eggs, vanilla and milk into a large bowl and beat together until smooth. Divide the mixture in half and put one half into another bowl. Mix the dried raspberries, raspberry extract and pink food colouring into one batter until a pink colour. Mix the lemon extract and yellow food colouring into the other batter until you get a nice bright yellow colour.

Spoon each mixture into a prepared tin and bake in the oven for 25–30 minutes, or until a skewer inserted into the centres comes out clean. Leave to cool in the tins.

Heat the raspberry preserve in a small saucepan until runny, then pass through a sieve into a bowl. Trim the sponges, each to the same width as the sponge height, to form 4 identical long rectangles, 2 from each colour (freeze any leftover sponge for another time). Using a patterned rolling pin on a work surface lightly dusted with icing sugar, roll out the white modelling chocolate to a rectangle, 25 x 20cm (10 x 8in).

Place a pink and yellow sponge rectangle side by side, brushing preserve in between them to stick together. Brush some preserve over the top, then place the remaining pink and yellow sponges on top, alternating the colours and sticking together with more preserve. Brush the outside of the sponges with preserve but not the cut ends.

Carefully place the stacked sponge in the centre of the modelling chocolate, then tightly wrap the chocolate around the cake. Turn it over so that it is seam side down and trim off any excess. Dust a few fresh raspberries with icing sugar and arrange on top to decorate.

DECADENT CHOCOLATE PAVLOVA

I discovered the pavlova when I arrived in the UK and ever since I have been creating new versions of this versatile, delicious dessert. This is my latest – a chocolate version, of course!

SERVES 10

Preparation time: 25 minutes,
  plus cooling
Cooking time: 1 hour 45 minutes

6 egg whites
350g (11½oz) golden caster sugar
1 tbsp cornflour
4 tbsp pure cocoa powder
1 tsp white wine vinegar
100g (3½oz) dark chocolate chips
100g (3½oz) white chocolate
  chips
100g (3½oz) mini marshmallows
500ml (17fl oz) whipping cream
2 tsp vanilla extract
50g (2oz) dark chocolate, finely
  grated
icing sugar, for dusting

Preheat the oven to 120°C (fan 100°C)/250°F/gas mark ½.
Line a large baking sheet with baking paper.

In a large, clean, dry bowl, whisk the egg whites to stiff peaks, adding the sugar a little at a time. Sift the cornflour and cocoa powder together, then gently fold into the egg whites with the vinegar until combined. Fold in the chocolate chips and marshmallows but do not over-mix.

Using a rubber spatula, spread some of the mixture on to the prepared baking sheet to form a 22cm (8½in) diameter disc, then pile high with the remaining mixture.

Bake in the oven for 1 hour 45 minutes, or until crunchy on the outside and gooey in the centre. Leave on the paper and transfer to a cooling rack to cool completely. It will sink and crack a little.

Whip the cream and vanilla together to firm peaks, then pile high on the meringue. Dust with the grated chocolate and icing sugar. Serve immediately.

TIP

Use a baking sheet that is large enough to allow a 22cm (8½in) diameter meringue to expand during cooking.

CHOCOLATE FONDANTS WITH ORANGE AND MUSCAT COMPOTE

Sinfully sweet and intensely indulgent, this recipe is a chocoholic's dream!
The orange compote marries the classic chocolate and orange combination.

SERVES 4

Preparation time: 15 minutes
Cooking time: 15 minutes

2 tsp cocoa powder
125g (4oz) unsalted butter,
  plus extra for greasing
200g (7oz) dark chocolate,
  roughly chopped
75g (3oz) golden caster sugar
2 eggs, plus 2 egg yolks
25g (1oz) plain flour

For the orange compote
1 large orange, peeled and
  segmented
2 tsp golden caster sugar
1 tsp cornflour
100ml (3½fl oz) muscat wine

Preheat the oven to 180°C (fan 160°C)/350°F/gas mark 4. Grease 4 x 150ml (¼ pint) individual pudding moulds, then coat with the cocoa powder, tapping out any excess. Transfer the moulds to a baking sheet.

Melt the chocolate and butter together in a heatproof bowl set over a pan of barely simmering water, making sure the surface of the water does not touch the bowl, stirring until smooth. Leave to cool for a few minutes.

In a large bowl, whisk the sugar, eggs and egg yolks together using an electric hand whisk until thick, pale and fluffy and doubled in volume. Gently stir the cooled chocolate into the mixture, then fold in the flour.

Divide the mixture between the prepared pudding moulds, filling them three-quarters full. Cook in the oven for 12 minutes.

Meanwhile, make the orange compote. Put the orange segments into a frying pan and heat gently, then stir in the sugar and cook gently until the mixture starts to sizzle. Mix the cornflour with a little water to a paste, then add with the wine to the oranges and cook until the compote has reduced by half.

Remove the fondants from the oven and use a sharp knife to slide around the edge of each pudding mould to release. Invert on to 4 plates and carefully remove the moulds. Serve immediately with the orange compote.

MINI CHOCOLATE SYRUP CAKES

Theses cute puddings are perfect winter warmers and a great ending to a long, lazy Sunday lunch. The amaretto gives them a delicious continental touch. Best served with a dark chocolate sauce (see page 120).

SERVES 6

Preparation time: 25 minutes
Cooking time: 25–30 minutes

100g (3½oz) unsalted butter, plus extra for greasing
100g (3½oz) dark chocolate, roughly chopped
2 eggs
50g (2oz) dark muscovado sugar
40g (1½oz) golden syrup
75g (3oz) ground almonds
15g (½oz) plain flour, plus extra for dusting
½ tsp baking powder
2 tbsp amaretto liqueur
6 amaretti biscuits, plus extra to decorate

Grease 6 x 150ml (¼ pint) individual pudding moulds and dust with flour, tapping out any excess. Cut out 6 small circles of baking paper to fit the bases and drop one into each mould. Grease 6 pieces of foil, each about 15cm (6in) square.

Put the butter and chocolate into a saucepan and heat gently until melted. Leave to cool.

Whisk the eggs, sugar and golden syrup together in a large bowl using an electric hand whisk until thick and foamy. Fold in the cooled chocolate mixture using a rubber spatula. Mix the ground almonds, flour and baking powder together in a separate bowl, then fold into the mixture with 1 tablespoon of the amaretto.

Preheat the oven to 200°C (fan 180°C)/400°F/gas mark 6.

Put the biscuits in a small bowl and splash over the remaining amaretto. Fill the prepared pudding moulds one-third full with cake mixture, then drop a soaked biscuit into each. Top with the remaining mixture, leaving 1cm (½in) between the mixture and the top of the moulds. Loosely scrunch a foil square over the top of each mould.

Put the moulds into a roasting tin and pour in hot water to come about halfway up the sides of the moulds. Bake in the oven for 20–25 minutes, or until a skewer inserted into the centres comes out clean.

To serve the puddings, use a sharp knife to slide around the edge of each pudding mould to release. Invert on to plates and carefully remove the moulds. Spoon over some chocolate sauce, allowing it to drizzle over the edges, then sprinkle with broken amaretti biscuits. Serve immediately.

TRUFFLES
AND TREATS

OLD-FASHIONED DUSTED TRUFFLES

I have fond memories of this simple but delicious recipe. As kids we spent hours making truffles for the festive season. By the end we were covered head to toe with cocoa powder, but it was still great fun to make them. These are fresh truffles and need to be kept in the refrigerator and consumed within 1 week – that's if you can resist eating them straight away!

MAKES 30

Preparation time: 15 minutes, plus chilling
Cooking time: 5 minutes

250g (8oz) dark chocolate, chopped
2 tbsp milk
1 tbsp espresso coffee
100g (3½oz) unsalted butter, softened
2 egg yolks
25g (1oz) cocoa powder, sifted

Gently melt the chocolate and milk together in a heatproof bowl set over a saucepan of barely simmering water, making sure the surface of the water does not touch the bowl.

Remove from the heat and stir in the coffee, butter and egg yolks until combined. Transfer the mixture to a bowl and leave to set in the refrigerator for 4 hours.

Place the cocoa powder on a plate. Using a dessertspoon, scoop out spoonfuls of the chocolate mixture. Coat your hands in cocoa powder to prevent the mixture from sticking and roll the chocolate mixture between the palms of your hand to form walnut-sized balls.

Using a fork, roll the truffles in the cocoa powder to coat. Store the truffles in an airtight container in the refrigerator for up to 1 week.

TIP

It is best to remove the truffles from the refrigerator and bring to room temperature before serving.

PINK FIZZ CHAMPAGNE TRUFFLES

If like me you like rosé champagne and chocolate, this after-dinner truffle with extra pop will be your new favourite treat.

MAKES 15

Preparation time: 15 minutes, plus chilling
Cooking time: 5 minutes

100g (3½oz) dark chocolate, chopped
100ml (3½fl oz) single cream
2 tsp Marc de Champagne
2 tsp plain popping candy
5 tbsp icing sugar
1 tsp pink food colouring

Put the chocolate into a heatproof bowl. Put the cream into a small saucepan and heat until steaming hot, but do not let it boil, then pour on to the chocolate and stir gently until melted, smooth and glossy. Leave to cool.

When cooled, stir in the champagne, then the popping candy. Leave to set in the refrigerator for at least 4 hours.

Put the icing sugar and food colouring into a blender and whizz together. Tip on to a plate.

Using a teaspoon, scoop up the ganache and roll between the palms of your hand to form perfect round shapes. Using a fork, roll the truffles in the pink icing sugar to coat. Store the truffles in an airtight container in the refrigerator for up to 1 week.

TIP

Dust your hands with icing sugar before rolling the truffles to stop the ganache sticking.

CRISP CHOCOLATE BONBONS

Very crunchy, very nutty and, of course, very chocolaty; theses sweets make a perfect gift wrapped in cellophane wrappers and placed in a beautiful glass jar.

MAKES 24

Preparation time: 15 minutes,
plus cooling and chilling
Cooking time: 5 minutes

200g (7oz) milk chocolate,
roughly chopped
200ml (7fl oz) crème fraîche
50g (2oz) crispy rice cereal
50g (2oz) nibbed almonds,
roasted (see Tip on page 26)
50g (2oz) chopped hazelnuts,
roasted (see Tip on page 26)

Line a 19cm (7½in) square shallow baking tin with baking paper.

Melt the chocolate in a heatproof bowl set over a saucepan of barely simmering water until smooth and glossy, making sure the surface of the water does not touch the bowl. Meanwhile, put the crème fraîche into a saucepan and heat gently, then stir into the melted chocolate. Leave to cool.

Divide the chocolate mixture between 3 small bowls and stir one of the dry ingredients into each.

Spoon the coated crispy rice cereal into the prepared tin and press down with the back of a spoon. Leave to set in the refrigerator.

Once set, spread the coated almonds over the top, then return to the refrigerator and leave to set.

Repeat with the hazelnut mixture to form 3 layers, then cover with clingfilm and chill in the refrigerator for at least 4 hours until completely set.

Remove from the tin on to a chopping board and cut into 24 small rectangles using a large, sharp knife. Wrap the bonbons in sweet wrapping paper. Store in an airtight container for up to 1 week.

LARGE HAZELNUT BOUCHÉES

Bouchées are large chocolate treats, which you usually graze on throughout the day, making the indulgent pleasure last even longer.

MAKES 36

Preparation time: 30 minutes, plus cooling, chilling and setting
Cooking time: 20 minutes

For the filling
150g (5oz) hazelnuts
125g (4oz) golden caster sugar
butter, for greasing
75g (3oz) milk chocolate, roughly chopped
25g (1oz) dark chocolate, roughly chopped

For the coating
100g (3½oz) dark chocolate, roughly chopped
100g (3½oz) milk chocolate, roughly chopped
25g (1oz) nibbed almonds, roasted (see Tip on page 26)
a couple of pinches of coarse sea salt crystals

First make the filling. Preheat the oven to 180°C (fan 160°C)/350°F/gas mark 4. Place the hazelnuts on a baking sheet and roast in the oven for 10 minutes until lightly golden.

Meanwhile, put the sugar into a heavy-based saucepan and heat until it forms a dark caramel, then stir in the roasted hazelnuts and turn on to a greased baking sheet. Leave to cool completely.

When cool, break the brittle into smaller pieces and place in a blender, then whizz to a fine powder.

Melt the milk chocolate and dark chocolate together in a heatproof bowl set over a saucepan of barely simmering water, making sure the surface of the water does not touch the bowl. Remove from the heat and stir in the hazelnut powder, mixing to a smooth, thick paste.

Using a teaspoon, fill a silicone round-shaped chocolate mould with the mixture and leave to set in the refrigerator. When completely set, carefully remove the chocolates from the moulds. (The filling makes about 36 chocolates, so you may have to make these in batches.)

To coat the bouchées, melt both chocolates together in a heatproof bowl as above, then remove from the heat and stir in the almonds and salt. Using a fork, dip the chocolate balls into the melted chocolate to coat completely, tapping off any excess. Place on a sheet of baking paper or acetate and leave to set. Store in an airtight container for up to 1 week.

HONEY AND MILK CHOCOLATE BARS

Kids are usually fonder of milk and white chocolate so what could be more fun than making your own treats before eating them? This easy-to-make recipe will be a hit with adults, too.

SERVES 8

Preparation time: 10 minutes, plus chilling
Cooking time: 10 minutes

200g (7oz) milk chocolate, roughly chopped, plus an extra 25g (1oz) for the topping
40g (1½oz) unsalted butter, plus extra for greasing
2 tbsp clear honey
2 tbsp condensed milk
75g (3oz) crispy rice cereal
25g (1oz) desiccated coconut
150g (5oz) white chocolate, roughly chopped

Grease an 18cm (7in) square shallow baking tin and line with baking paper.

Put the milk chocolate, butter, honey and condensed milk into a small saucepan and heat gently until melted and smooth, then stir in the crispy rice cereal and coconut.

Spoon the mixture into the prepared tin and level the top with the back of a spoon. Leave to set in the refrigerator for at least 30 minutes.

Melt the white chocolate in a heatproof bowl set over a saucepan of barely simmering water, making sure the surface of the water does not touch the bowl. Leave to cool for a few minutes, then spread over the top of the rice cake. Return to the refrigerator to set.

Melt the remaining 25g (1oz) of milk chocolate as above, then spoon the chocolate into a small piping bag with a small hole snipped at the tip. Drizzle a pattern over the white chocolate and leave to set at room temperature.

Remove from the tin on to a chopping board and cut into rectangular bars using a large, sharp knife. Store in an airtight container or wrap in cellophane bags for gifts.

TIP

This is an easy recipe for kids to make but will require adult supervision and help, especially when cutting the fridge cake into bars with the sharp knife!

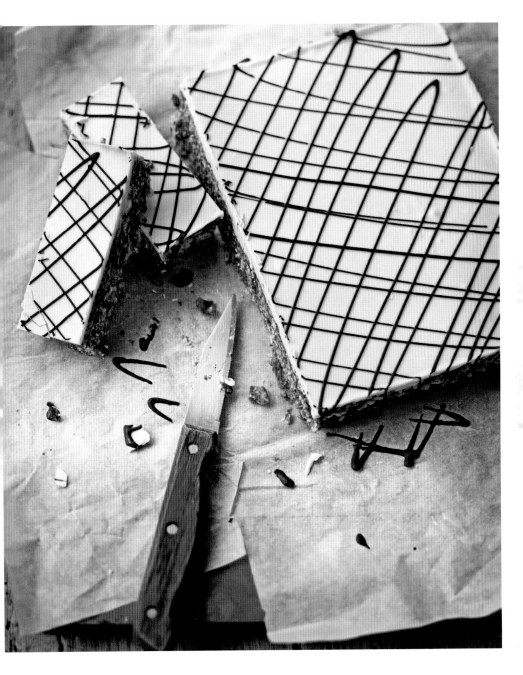

CHOCOLATE GUIMAUVE

Marshmallows have made a huge comeback and are no longer just for kids. Gourmet mallows are everywhere and these chocolate ones are definitely for grown-ups.

MAKES 45 SQUARES

Preparation time: 25 minutes, plus chilling
Cooking time: 10 minutes

50g (2oz) cocoa powder
150ml (¼ pint) water
2 tsp amaretto liqueur
200g (7oz) golden caster sugar
2 tbsp gelatine powder
2 tsp vanilla paste
125ml (4fl oz) corn syrup
125g (4oz) dark chocolate, roughly chopped

Line a 20cm (8in) square, 6cm (2½in) deep baking tin with baking paper, then dust generously with some of the cocoa powder.

Put the water, amaretto, sugar and gelatine powder into a small saucepan over a low heat and stir until it has dissolved but do not let it boil. Remove from the heat and stir in the vanilla paste.

Transfer the mixture to the bowl of a free-standing mixer, add the corn syrup and whisk to stiff peaks – this may take up to 12 minutes.

Meanwhile, melt the chocolate in a heatproof bowl set over a saucepan of barely simmering water, making sure the surface of the water does not touch the bowl. Leave to cool for a few minutes, then fold into the whisked mallow.

Pour the mixture into the prepared tin and spread level using a damp palette knife. Leave to set in the refrigerator for at least 1 hour.

Dust a chopping board with some more of the cocoa powder and sift the remaining cocoa powder into a shallow bowl. Turn out the mallow on to the board, then cut into bite-sized cubes. Using a fork, roll the mallows in the sifted cocoa powder, shaking off the excess. Store in an airtight container for up to 2 weeks.

CHOCOLATE HONEYCOMB

I love offering these rough shards of sweet honeycomb as gifts wrapped up in cellophane. They are great to eat on their own or to crumble on ice cream.

MAKES 1 X 20CM (8IN) SQUARE

Preparation time: 10 minutes, plus setting
Cooking time: 8 minutes

unsalted butter, for greasing
200g (7oz) golden caster sugar
4 tbsp golden syrup
25g (1oz) dark chocolate, finely chopped
1 tbsp bicarbonate of soda

Grease a 20cm (8in) square shallow baking tin.

Melt the sugar and golden syrup together in a heavy-based saucepan over a low heat, then increase the heat to medium and simmer for 3–4 minutes, or until the mixture is thick and a dark caramel colour.

Remove from the heat, add the chocolate and immediately whisk in the bicarbonate of soda so that the mixture froths up – stand back just in case.

Pour the mixture into the prepared tin and leave to set at room temperature for about 2–3 hours.

Remove from the tin and break into large pieces using a rolling pin. Store in cellophane bags for up to 1 week.

TIP

To make the honeycomb more luxurious, drizzle some melted white and milk chocolate on the top of the pieces before serving or wrapping them.

CHOCOLATE FUDGE

I had never come across fudge before I arrived in the UK, but it didn't take me long to become fond of these sweets eaten mostly on trips to seaside towns. They make such a great gift when beautifully wrapped.

MAKES 36

Preparation time: 10 minutes,
plus chilling
Cooking time: 5 minutes

400g (13oz) dark chocolate,
roughly chopped
400ml can condensed milk
25g (1oz) unsalted butter, plus
extra for greasing
100g (3½oz) golden icing sugar

Lightly grease a 19cm (7½in) square shallow baking tin.

Put the chocolate, condensed milk and butter into a small saucepan and melt gently over a low heat, stirring occasionally, until smooth and silky. Sift in the icing sugar and mix thoroughly.

Press the mixture into the prepared tin and smooth over the top with the back of a spoon. Cover with clingfilm and leave to set in the refrigerator for 1 hour.

Turn out the fudge on to a chopping board and cut into 36 squares. Store in an airtight container in a cool, dry place for up to 1 week.

TIP

For variety, try adding chopped nuts or dried fruits to the mixture.

CHOCOLATE ORANGE TRUFFLES

When you hear about the popular combination of chocolate and orange you always think dark chocolate, but it does work surprisingly well with white chocolate too, if not better.

MAKES 24

Preparation time: 40 minutes,
  plus chilling and setting
Cooking time: 8 minutes

75ml (3fl oz) double cream
500g (1lb) white chocolate,
  chopped
25g (1oz) unsalted butter
4 tsp orange liqueur
50g (2oz) candied orange peel,
  finely chopped
50g (2oz) dark chocolate,
  roughly chopped

Put the cream into a small saucepan and heat to just below boiling point. Stir in half of the white chocolate and the butter until smooth. Add the liqueur and orange peel, then transfer the mixture to a bowl and leave to firm up in the refrigerator.

Line a baking sheet with baking paper. Using a teaspoon, scoop up small amounts of the ganache, shape into balls with your hands and place on the baking sheet.

Melt the remaining white chocolate in a heatproof bowl set over a saucepan of barely simmering water, making sure the surface of the water does not touch the bowl. Leave to cool for a few minutes.

Using a fork, dip each ganache ball into the melted white chocolate, then return to the lined baking sheet and leave to set.

Melt the dark chocolate as above and leave to cool for a few minutes. Spoon the melted dark chocolate into a small piping bag fitted with a very thin piping nozzle, then pipe fine lines on to each truffle and leave to set. Store the truffles in an airtight container in a cool, dry place for up to 1 week.

TIP

If the balls of ganache soften before you are ready to dip them in the melted white chocolate, place them in the refrigerator to firm up, or place them in the freezer for 10 minutes.

SOFT CHOCOLATE BUTTER TOFFEE

Brittany, where I grew up, is the only region of France that uses salted butter for everyday use. Toffee is one of those sweets that work so well with a little bit of salt added, too.

MAKES 25

Preparation time: 20 minutes, plus setting overnight
Cooking time: 20 minutes

oil, for greasing
50g (2oz) dark chocolate, 99% cocoa solids or the darkest you can get, roughly chopped
4 tsp water
100g (3½oz) glucose syrup
250g (8oz) golden caster sugar
100g (3½oz) salted butter
200ml (7fl oz) double cream

Lightly oil a 20cm (8in) square shallow baking tin.

Melt the chocolate in a heatproof bowl set over a saucepan of barely simmering water, making sure the surface of the water does not touch the bowl.

Meanwhile, place the water, glucose and sugar in a heavy-based saucepan and heat over a medium heat until it forms a nice blond caramel. Remove from the heat and add 15g (½oz) of the butter to cool the mixture.

Put the cream into a small saucepan and heat slightly, then slowly pour it into the caramel, stirring gently. Add the remaining butter, return the pan to the heat and heat until the mixture reaches 118°C (244°F) on a sugar thermometer.

Remove from the heat and stir in the melted chocolate until smooth. Pour into the prepared tin and leave to cool and set at room temperature overnight.

Turn the toffee out on to a chopping board and cut into 25 small squares using a large knife. The toffees look nice stored in a jar or wrapped in colourful paper.

DRINKS, SPREADS & SAUCES

SPICY 'AZTEC' HOT CHOCOLATE

This is probably the oldest known hot chocolate recipe. The Aztecs used this spicy drink to give them power when going into battle. The combination of the dark chocolate and spices makes it a proper pick-me-up elixir – drink this and you will be ready to face any battle!

SERVES 4

Preparation time: 5 minutes
Cooking time: 5 minutes

1 litre (1¾ pints) milk
100g (3½oz) dark chocolate,
   roughly chopped
2 tbsp light muscovado sugar
1 tsp ground cinnamon
1 tsp freshly grated nutmeg
1 tsp ground black pepper
100ml (3½fl oz) whipping cream
ground cinnamon and freshly
   grated nutmeg, for dusting

Put the milk into a heavy-based saucepan and bring to the boil. Reduce the heat, then add the chocolate, sugar and spices.
....
Using a small balloon whisk, whisk until the chocolate has completely melted. Simmer for 1 minute, then remove from the heat and whisk in the cream.
....
Pour into tall mugs and serve with a dusting of cinnamon and grated nutmeg.

CHOCOLATE MARTINI

There is something special about starting an evening with a martini. This chocolate version will surprise and amaze your guests, but watch out as it is a very easy-to-drink concoction...

SERVES 1

Preparation time: 5 minutes,
  plus chilling

1 tbsp finely grated dark chocolate
50ml (2fl oz) whipping cream
1½ shots (60ml/2½fl oz) Irish
  cream liqueur
1½ shots (60ml/2½fl oz) crème
  de cacao
½ shot (20ml/1fl oz) vodka
ice cubes

First prepare your glass. Using your fingertip, wet the rim of the glass with water. Scatter the grated chocolate on a small plate and turn the glass in the chocolate to coat the rim. Chill in the refrigerator and reserve the remaining chocolate.

When ready to serve, lightly whip the cream until thickened slightly but still very sloppy. Put all the alcohol into a cocktail shaker with some ice cubes. Shake well, then pour it into the chilled glass and add a twirl of the cream. Finish with a sprinkle of the reserved chocolate and serve immediately. Santé!

CHOCOLATE CARAMEL COCKTAIL

This is my favourite winter cocktail to serve to friends. It is very moreish – drink in moderation.

SERVES 3–4

Preparation time: 10 minutes,
  plus chilling
Cooking time: 5 minutes

15g (½oz) cocoa powder, plus 1 tsp
1 tsp sugar syrup
50g (2oz) golden caster sugar
4 tsp water
250ml (8fl oz) single cream
50ml (2fl oz) crème de cacao
50ml (2fl oz) orange liqueur
ice cubes

First prepare your glasses. Place the 1 teaspoon of cocoa powder and sugar syrup on separate saucers. Dip the rim of each glass into the syrup and then into the cocoa powder. Chill in the refrigerator.

Put the sugar and water into a heavy-based saucepan and heat gently until the sugar has dissolved, then increase the heat and cook until it forms a nice dark blond caramel. Add the cream and whisk in, scraping up the caramel from the bottom of the pan. Add the remaining cocoa powder and cook for a further 2 minutes, or until smooth. Pass through a sieve into a blender to remove any caramel pieces, then add both liqueurs and blend for few minutes. Chill in the refrigerator.

When ready to serve, place some ice cubes in a cocktail shaker with the chilled cocktail and shake well. Pass through a cocktail sieve, pour into the chilled glasses and serve immediately.

DOUBLE CHOCOLATE MILKSHAKE

This version of a classic chocolate milkshake reminds me of the first time I ate in a proper diner in the USA and had my first milkshake. A good shake should be creamy, thick and smooth, and leave you full – it's almost a dessert in a glass.

SERVES 4

Preparation time: 5 minutes,
  plus chilling
Cooking time: 3 minutes

1 litre (1¾ pints) milk
100g (3½oz) dark chocolate,
  roughly chopped
4 large scoops of good-quality
  chocolate ice cream
2 tsp chocolate extract
2 tbsp malted milk powder
20 ice cubes
good-quality drinking chocolate
  powder, for dusting

Chill 4 tall serving glasses in the refrigerator.

Put the milk into a saucepan and heat to simmering point. Remove from the heat, add the chocolate and stir until completely melted. Leave to cool, then chill in the refrigerator for 10 minutes.

Pour the chocolate milk into a blender with the remaining ingredients. Blend at full speed until the mixture is light and frothy and there are no more ice crystals.

Pour into the chilled glasses, dust generously with drinking chocolate powder and serve immediately. Sit back and enjoy…

CHOCOLATE AND COLA FLOAT

This is a reminder of those great soda parlours where as kids we were treated to fabulous Sunday outings. For me, the best treat was the cola float, as we never drank cola at home, so it was a double celebration! I wish soda parlours would make a comeback. In the meantime, try this updated recipe.

SERVES 4

Preparation time: 10 minutes, plus chilling

250ml (8fl oz) double cream
1 litre (1¾ pints) cola (preferably the old-fashioned type)
2 tsp vanilla extract or paste
8 scoops of dark chocolate ice cream
100g (3½oz) maraschino cherries, plus a few extra to decorate
25g (1oz) dark chocolate, grated

Chill 4 tall sundae glasses in the refrigerator.
....
When ready to serve, lightly whip the cream until thickened slightly but still sloppy. Put to one side.
....
Put the cola, vanilla, ice cream and cherries into a large blender, in 2 batches if necessary, and use the pulse button to blend together.
....
Pour into the chilled glasses, spoon the cream on top and sprinkle over the grated chocolate. Decorate with a few maraschino cherries for a little touch of kitsch and serve immediately.

TIP
....
It is best to use the pulse button when blending the cola float, as it will fizz and froth a lot.

CONQUISTADORS' HOT COCOA

The conquistadors were responsible for introducing cocoa to Europe and this version of hot chocolate is also known as Spanish chocolate. I've added some Seville orange to it for an Iberian touch. This rich drink is best served with churros, the long Spanish doughnuts. A warning though – you can get hooked!

SERVES 6–8

Preparation time: 5 minutes
Cooking time: 10 minutes

250ml (8fl oz) water
100g (3½oz) light muscovado
  sugar
2 tbsp cornflour
75g (3oz) cocoa powder
500ml (17fl oz) milk
grated zest of 1 orange
  (Seville if in season)
1 tsp vanilla paste or extract
1 tsp pure orange extract
  (optional)

Put the water and sugar into a heavy-based saucepan and bring to the boil, stirring until the sugar has completely dissolved. Remove from the heat, sift the cornflour and cocoa powder together and whisk into the syrup using a small balloon whisk.

Return the pan to the heat and cook until the mixture forms a thick paste. Add the milk a little at a time, whisking continuously until smooth and glossy, then add the grated orange zest, vanilla and orange extract, if using. Simmer for 5 minutes, stirring continuously.

Serve piping hot in small warm coffee cups.

TIP

For a grown-up version, replace the orange extract with orange liqueur.

AFTER-DINNER MINT HOT CHOCOLATE

It is almost a tradition to serve after-dinner mint chocolates but why not serve a hot mint chocolate instead to impress your guests? It's one of my favourite dinner party tricks.

SERVES 14–16

Preparation time: 10 minutes
Cooking time: 10 minutes

200g (7oz) light muscovado sugar
100g (3½oz) boiled mint sweets
500ml (17fl oz) water
125g (4oz) cocoa powder
2 tbsp cornflour
500ml (17fl oz) milk

Place the sugar and mint sweets in a food processor and blend to a fine powder. Put the water and sugar powder into a heavy-based saucepan and bring to the boil, stirring until the sugar powder has dissolved. Remove from the heat, sift the cocoa powder and cornflour together and whisk into the syrup using a small balloon whisk.

Return the pan to the heat and simmer until the mixture forms a smooth paste. Add the milk a little at a time, whisking until the mixture is smooth and glossy. Serve immediately in small heatproof shot glasses.

PROPER ITALIAN HOT CHOCOLATE

When growing up, my family went to a ski resort a few miles from Turin and my treat was this phenomenal thick hot chocolate called cioccolata calda. Legend says: 'if your spoon doesn't stand up in your cup, it is not a proper one', but even I haven't managed to get mine to that status!

SERVES 6–8

Preparation time: 5 minutes
Cooking time: 15 minutes

1 litre (1¾ pints) milk
100g (3½oz) light muscovado sugar
100g (3½oz) cocoa powder
150ml (¼ pint) crème fraîche
2 tsp vanilla paste or extract

Put the milk and sugar into a heavy-based saucepan and heat gently until the sugar has dissolved. Remove from the heat and whisk in the cocoa powder and crème fraîche.

Return to a low heat and bring to a simmer, stirring. Simmer for about 10 minutes, or until thickened. Add the vanilla and whisk until frothy. Serve in small warm cups.

MOCHA BRÛLÉE

This extraordinary drink is a fantastic party piece that needs a little preparation but is worth all the effort.

SERVES 4

Preparation time: 10 minutes
Cooking time: 5 minutes

800ml (1 pint 7fl oz) milk
4 shots of espresso coffee
  made with 200ml (7fl oz)
  just-boiled water
8 tbsp dark drinking chocolate
  powder
2 tsp vanilla paste or extract
4 tbsp demerara sugar

Put the milk into a saucepan and heat to just below boiling point.

Put the coffee into a heatproof bowl, add the drinking chocolate powder and stir until blended. Using a small balloon whisk, add 600ml (1 pint) of the hot milk a little at a time until the mixture is smooth. Stir in the vanilla, then pour into 4 warm flameproof coffee cups or small mugs.

Using an electric milk frother, froth the remaining hot milk. Spoon on top of the coffees and level it flat with a knife. Sprinkle the sugar over the froth in each glass and caramelize using a kitchen blowtorch. Serve immediately.

TIP

Skimmed milk froths more easily than semi-skimmed or full-fat milk.

VIENNESE CHOCOLATE

Vienna is known as the world capital of the coffee shop, where for hundreds of years they've served speciality coffee, pastries and other hot drinks. Viennese chocolate is certainly one of their most famous treats – pure indulgence in a glass.

SERVES 4

Preparation time: 10 minutes
Cooking time: 10 minutes

200g (7oz) dark chocolate, roughly chopped
100ml (3½fl oz) whipping cream
25g (1oz) icing sugar
2 tsp vanilla sugar
1 litre (1¾ pints) milk
4 tbsp light muscovado sugar
cocoa powder and ground cinnamon, for dusting

Melt the chocolate in a heatproof bowl set over a saucepan of barely simmering water, making sure the surface of the water does not touch the bowl.

Meanwhile, whip the cream, icing sugar and vanilla sugar to stiff peaks and put to one side.

Put the milk and muscovado sugar into a saucepan and heat gently until the sugar has dissolved. Whisk in the melted chocolate a little at the time, then whisk over a low heat for at least 5 minutes, or until the mixture is smooth and glossy.

Pour the hot chocolate into 4 tall warm latte glasses. Scoop the cream nice and high on the tops, lightly dust with cocoa powder and cinnamon and serve immediately.

HAZELNUT AND CHOCOLATE SPREAD

You can never beat homemade products and this spread is the absolute proof. It's a perfect breakfast treat when spread generously on toasted brioche.

MAKES 2 X 450G (1LB) JARS

Preparation time: 5 minutes, plus cooling
Cooking time: 10 minutes

100g (3½oz) ground hazelnuts
150g (5oz) dark chocolate, roughly chopped
250g (8oz) unsalted butter
2 tsp vanilla paste or extract
400ml can condensed milk
2 tbsp hazelnut oil

Preheat the oven to 180°C (fan 160°C)/350°F/gas mark 4. Spread the ground hazelnuts on a baking sheet and roast for 3–4 minutes, or until a nice rich golden colour and the full aroma escapes from the oven. Leave to cool.

Melt the chocolate and one-quarter of the butter together in a small heatproof bowl set over a saucepan of barely simmering water, making sure the surface of the water does not touch the bowl. When melted, remove the saucepan from the heat but leave the bowl over the hot water. Stir in the roasted hazelnuts and the remaining ingredients until the mixture is smooth and glossy.

Pour into sterilized pots or jars (see Tip below), then leave to cool completely before sealing. Store in the refrigerator for up to 2 weeks. This is best removed from the refrigerator 1 hour before serving.

WHITE CHOCOLATE SPREAD

This rich, luxurious white chocolate spread is perfect with toasted gingerbread or malt loaf.

MAKES ABOUT 300ML (½ PINT)

Preparation time: 5 minutes
Cooking time: 5 minutes

200g (7oz) white chocolate, roughly chopped
150ml (¼ pint) canned condensed milk
2 tsp vanilla paste
50ml (2fl oz) single cream

Melt all the ingredients together until smooth and glossy in a large heatproof bowl set over a saucepan of barely simmering water, making sure the surface of the water does not touch the bowl.

Pour into small, sterilized jars (see Tip), then leave to cool completely before sealing. Store in the refrigerator for up to 2 weeks.

TIP

To sterilize jars, put clean, washed and dried jars into a cold oven with the lids off. Heat the oven to 180°C (fan 160°C)/350°F/gas mark 4 and leave for 20 minutes. Pour your chocolate spread into the jars while still warm from the oven.

CHOCOLATE FONDUE

I know fondue is a bit retro, but a good chocolate fondue is a great alternative to a dessert or perfect for a party. You can be as creative as you want with the food to be dipped.

SERVES 6

Preparation time: 15 minutes
Cooking time: 5 minutes

300g (10oz) dark chocolate,
  roughly chopped
2 tbsp milk
250ml (8fl oz) double cream
75g (3oz) unsalted butter,
  softened
1 tsp ground cinnamon
1 tsp vanilla paste or extract
2 tbsp dark rum

For dipping and coating
3 bananas, cut into chunky
  pieces
3 ripe pears, peeled, cored and
  cut into chunky pieces
juice of 1 lemon
12 large marshmallows
assortment of dried fruit, such
  as figs, dates and prunes
150g (5oz) chopped hazelnuts,
  roasted (see Tip on page 26)
150g (5oz) desiccated coconut

First prepare the dips. Toss the bananas and pears with the lemon juice to prevent browning. Arrange the prepared fruit, marshmallow and dried fruit on a large platter or in ramekins, together with the roasted nuts and coconut. Make a pile of metal or wooden kebab sticks on the side.

To make the fondue, place a fondue pan in a bain-marie. Alternatively, place a heatproof serving bowl over a saucepan of simmering water. Add the chocolate and milk and melt together, then whisk in the cream. Keep warm, then just before serving stir in the butter, cinnamon, vanilla and rum.

Take the warm fondue to the table hot and encourage people to help themselves. Use the kebab sticks to dip the fruits and marshmallows into the hot chocolate, then roll into the nuts or coconut. A fun way to end a dinner party!

FOUR ULTIMATE CHOCOLATE SAUCES

Chocolate sauces are a perfect accompaniment to desserts, crêpes, waffles and ice cream. Here I've penned four of my favourite ones.

DARK CHOCOLATE SAUCE

MAKES 500ML (17FL OZ)

Preparation time: 5 minutes
Cooking time: 2 minutes

125ml (4fl oz) milk
125ml (4fl oz) single cream
50g (2oz) golden caster sugar
200g (7oz) dark chocolate, chopped
50g (2oz) unsalted butter, softened

Put the milk, cream and sugar into a saucepan and heat gently until the sugar has dissolved. Remove from the heat and add the chocolate, stirring until melted. Stir in the butter. Serve warm on ice cream or over profiteroles, or chill, then serve cold with cake or crêpes.

IRISH CREAM CHOCOLATE SAUCE

Make the dark chocolate sauce as above, stirring in 3 tbsp Irish cream liqueur after adding the butter.

ZESTY WHITE CHOCOLATE SAUCE

MAKES ABOUT 300ML (½ PINT)

Preparation time: 5 minutes
Cooking time: 2 minutes

150ml (¼ pint) single cream
4 tbsp milk
200g (7oz) white chocolate, chopped
grated zest of 1 lemon
1 tbsp extra virgin olive oil

Put the cream and milk into a saucepan and bring to the boil. Remove from the heat and stir in the chocolate until melted and smooth, then stir in the lemon zest and olive oil. This superb combination is perfect for fruity, summery desserts.

MILK CHOCOLATE AND HAZELNUT SAUCE

MAKES ABOUT 300ML (½ PINT)

Preparation time: 5 minutes
Cooking time: 5 minutes

200g (7oz) milk chocolate, roughly chopped
75ml (3fl oz) single cream
1 tsp vanilla extract
2 tsp clear honey
25g (1oz) ground hazelnuts, roasted (see Tip on page 26)

Melt the chocolate in a heatproof bowl set over a saucepan of barely simmering water, making sure the surface of the water does not touch the bowl. Stir in the cream, vanilla and honey until smooth and glossy, then stir in the ground hazelnuts. Serve warm over ice cream, pancakes or fruit.

CHOCOLATE GLAZE

This is a perfect, delicious recipe to spread over cakes or treats like brownies. The easy glaze is rich, smooth and glossy, so it also works very well as a paint for those of you ready to express your artistic flair on fruit, plates or body parts!

**MAKES 150ML
(¼ PINT)**

Preparation time: 2 minutes
Cooking time: 3 minutes

125g (4oz) dark chocolate,
  roughly chopped
50g (2oz) unsalted butter
1 tbsp golden syrup
1 tsp vanilla extract or paste

Melt the chocolate, butter and golden syrup together in a heatproof bowl set over a saucepan of barely simmering water, making sure the surface of the water does not touch the bowl. Stir occasionally, until smooth and glossy, then add the vanilla.

Using a palette knife, spread the glaze over cakes or brownies.

TIP

If you are feeling artistic, decorate fruit and plates (or body parts!) with the chocolate glaze using a fine clean paintbrush.

INDEX

ABOUT THE AUTHOR

Eric Lanlard, Master Pâtissier and twice winner of the prestigious Continental Pâtissier of the Year at the British Baking Awards, has earned himself an international reputation for superlative baked creations for an impressive A-list clientele, including Madonna and Sir Elton John. Having trained in France, Eric moved to London where he ran the pâtisserie business for Albert and Michel Roux. He stayed there for five years before launching his own business, Cake Boy, a destination café, cake emporium and cookery school based in London.

Eric is an experienced TV presenter, and has presented two series' of Channel 4's *Baking Mad with Eric Lanlard*. He has also appeared on numerous TV food shows including *The Taste*, *Masterchef: The Professionals*, *Mary Queen of Shops*, *Great British Bake Off* and *Junior Bake Off*.

He is co-author of *Cox Cookies & Cake* (Mitchell Beazley) and author of *Master Cakes* (Hamlyn), *Home Bake*, *Tart It Up!* and *Chocolat* (Mitchell Beazley).